Keith Randell

Russia 1815–81

Russell Sherman

Hodder & Stoughton

A MEMBER OF THE HODDER HEADLINE GROUP

The cover illustration shows a Tsar Alexander I (courtesy of The Royal Society of Medicine).

Some other titles in the series:

Russia, Poland and the Ottoman Empire 1725–1800	ISBN 0 340 53334 X
Andrina Stiles	
Reaction and Revolutions: Russia 1881–1924	ISBN 0 340 53336 X
Michael Lynch	
Stalin and Khrushchev: The USSR 1924–64	ISBN 0 340 52559 2
Michael Lynch	
France in Revolution	ISBN 0 340 53494 X
Duncan Townson	
The Unification of Germany, 1815–70	ISBN 0 340 51810 3
Andrina Stiles	
The Unification of Italy, 1815–70	ISBN 0 340 51809 X
Andrina Stiles	
The Concert of Europe: International Relations 1815–70	ISBN 0 7131 7828 0
John Lowe	
Rivalry and Accord: International Relations 1870–1914	ISBN 0 340 51806 5
John Lowe	
France 1814–70: Monarchy, Republic and Empire	ISBN 0 340 51805 7
Keith Randell	
France: The Third Republic 1870–1914	ISBN 0 340 55569 6
Keith Randell	

British Library Cataloguing in Publication Data
Sherman, Russell
  Russia 1815–81. – (Access to history).
  1. Russia, 1794–
  I. Title   II. Series
  947.07

  ISBN 0 340 54789 8

First published 1991
Impression number 10   9   8   7   6   5   4
Year   1998   1997   1996   1995   1994

Typeset by Wearset, Boldon, Tyne and Wear
Printed in Great Britain for Hodder & Stoughton Educational, a division of Hodder Headline Plc, 338 Euston Road, London NW1 3BH by Page Bros, Norwich

Contents

Preface

To the general reader

Although the *Access to History* series has been designed with the needs of students studying the subject at higher examination levels very much in mind, it also has a great deal to offer the general reader. The main body of the text (i.e. ignoring the Study Guides at the ends of chapters) forms a readable and yet stimulating survey of a coherent topic as studied by historians. However, each author's aim has not merely been to provide a clear explanation of what happened in the past (to interest and inform): it has also been assumed that most readers wish to be stimulated into thinking further about the topic and to form opinions of their own about the significance of the events that are described and discussed (to be challenged). Thus, although no prior knowledge of the topic is expected on the reader's part, she or he is treated as an intelligent and thinking person throughout. The author tends to share ideas and possibilities with the reader, rather than passing on numbers of so-called 'historical truths'.

To the student reader

There are many ways in which the series can be used by students studying History at a higher level. It will, therefore, be worthwhile thinking about your own study strategy before you start your work on this book. Obviously, your strategy will vary depending on the aim you have in mind, and the time for study that is available to you.

If, for example, you want to acquire a general overview of the topic in the shortest possible time, the following approach will probably be the most effective:

1 Read Chapter 1 and think about its contents.
2 Read the 'Making notes' section at the end of Chapter 2 and decide whether it is necessary for you to read this chapter.
3 If it is, read the chapter, stopping at each heading or * to note down the main points that have been made.
4 Repeat stage 2 (and stage 3 where appropriate) for all the other chapters.

If, however, your aim is to gain a thorough grasp of the topic, taking however much time is necessary to do so, you may benefit from carrying out the same procedure with each chapter, as follows:

1 Read the chapter as fast as you can, and preferably at one sitting.
2 Study the flow diagram at the end of the chapter, ensuring that you understand the general 'shape' of what you have just read.

3   Read the 'Making notes' section (and the 'Answering essay questions' section, if there is one) and decide what further work you need to do on the chapter. In particularly important sections of the book, this will involve reading the chapter a second time and stopping at each heading and * to think about (and to write a summary of) what you have just read.

4   Attempt the 'Source-based questions' section. It will sometimes be sufficient to think through your answers, but additional understanding will often be gained by forcing yourself to write them down.

When you have finished the main chapters of the book, study the 'Further Reading' section and decide what additional reading (if any) you will do on the topic.

This book has been designed to help make your studies both enjoyable and successful. If you can think of ways in which this could have been done more effectively, please write to tell me. In the meantime, I hope that you will gain greatly from your study of History.

Keith Randell

CHAPTER 1

Russia in 1815

Russia is often seen as a European state. This can be misleading. To understand Russian history one must first understand how different Russia was from Europe, especially western Europe. Russia did not share the same intellectual, religious or social traditions. The Russian Orthodox Church was as distinct from the western churches as Rome was from Calvin. There was no tradition of the Tsar sharing power with any group. Even the Russian alphabet was distinct and different. Europe was important to Russia, but so were the vast territories to the east. The size of Russia alone distinguished her from her European contemporaries. The map on the next page was deliberately chosen to show a Russian perspective. It clearly demonstrates that she was far more than a European power. Russia was a vast sprawling empire made up of numerous nationalities. Her people were as diverse in language and culture as were the lands they inhabited. This disparate empire was held together by the autocratic power of the Tsars rather than by any natural bond between her peoples.

1 Russian Geography

A knowledge of Russian geography is central to an understanding of Russian development. In the late twentieth century it is rare for expert commentators to make more than a passing reference to the physical and climatic geography of a region, because in the developed world at least, modern technology has now overcome the majority of natural problems faced by societies. However, before these advances were made geography was often a major factor in determining the nature and scope of human activity. By 1815 Russia covered almost one sixth of the total land surface of the world. It stretched from the frozen wastes of the Arctic in the north to the arid deserts above Aghanistan in the south, and from central Europe in the west out towards Alaska in the east. However, the nature of this land and its climate placed severe limitations on its development and growth.

For one reason or another, very little of the land mass which comprised the Russian state could be called hospitable and productive. Russian vegetation can be divided into four main areas (see the map on page 4). The tundra to the north is too cold to support plant growth or unassisted human activity; the great forest zone, the taiga and wooded forest, is the largest forested area in the world; the steppe is a vast grassland plain which stretches from Hungary to Mongolia; and the semi-desert regions of Central Asia are unable to support large numbers of people.

There are two main areas fit for human habitation: the steppe and the

Periods of expansion

■	1260–1475
(dotted, darker)	15th century
(dotted, light)	16th century
(white)	17th century

(hatched)	18th century
(hatched)	19th century
- - - -	Present day

ALASKA 1789–1867

SAKHALIN

MANCHURIA

Vladivostok

Port Arthur 1898–1904

R. Amur

SIBERIA

R. Yenisey

Tomsk

R. Ob

URALS

TURKESTAN

TIEN SHAN

Archangel

Kazan

Astrakhan

CASPIAN SEA

KUBAN

R. Volga

BALTIC SEA

Novgorod

Moscow

Kiev

UKRAINE

R. Dnieper

BLACK SEA

0   1000 km

0   500 miles

The expansion of the Russian Empire

southern part of the forest region. These were described by Baron Haxthausen in the 1840s:

1 In the north of Russia the vegetation springs up into a forest; every fallow field, every uncultivated spot is covered with wood in a few years . . . in the Steppes, nature shoots up into grass and flowers; and what a luxuriant growth! Plants which are with us at
5 most two feet tall, here rise higher than the head.

This would appear to paint a picture of a rich and fertile land ready to be exploited. However, due to the nature of both soil and climate this is misleading. Russia's climate is what is called 'continental', being hot in summer but very cold in winter. The further east one progresses, the colder the winter becomes. Temperatures at Verkhoyansk in eastern Siberia have fallen as low as minus 90 degrees fahrenheit. As a result, much of eastern Siberia, on the same latitude as England, is impossible to cultivate. It also means that in the remainder the growing season is very short. Agricultural effort has to be concentrated into a very brief period in these areas. In the north of European Russia, which forms the core of the old Russian state, the land stays frozen for up to eight months a year. This factor, combined with uneven rainfall, led to one harvest in three being barely able to support the population. Rainfall is low in the most fertile areas of the black earth belt, but quite high in the sandy, less productive soils to the north-west. However, even here the rainfall is concentrated into the last two months of the growing season, so that it only has to be a few weeks late to cause severe problems.

* In the nineteenth century the result of these adverse conditions was low crop yields. By 1820 Russian wheat yields averaged 1 : 3 (three grains gathered for every one planted). In central Europe they averaged over 1:5, while in England they had already reached 1 : 8. This meant that the Russian peasant had very little surplus to meet the needs of a bad year, to eat, to sell, or to feed animals through the long winters. This in turn meant that there was little manure available to put life back into the soil, especially in the north where it was most needed.

However, these poor conditions cannot be blamed entirely on the adverse factors described above. In western Europe the growth of trade and cities had gone hand in hand with improvements in agriculture, one stimulating and reinforcing the other, providing the incentive for increased production. In Russia that incentive was lacking. The social and economic system did not allow the peasantry to reap the benefits of any increases in productivity. The limited progress which was being made was more than swallowed up by the rapid increase in population which took place after 1750. This population increase, coupled with the fact that the lack of an effective source of fertilizer meant that the

See Preface for explanation of * symbol.

The Russian Empire – vegetation and soil type

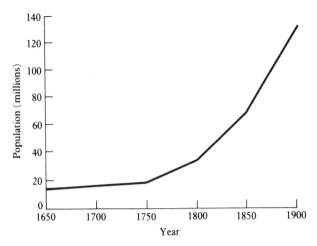

Russian population growth

fertility of land in the north was regularly exhausted, led to a continued expansion into new, still fertile, areas.

2 Social Structure

Russia was a rural state. About 96 per cent of the population lived in the countryside. The vast majority were peasants. The old social unit in Russia had been based on the extended family group, often numbering up to 50 or more people. By 1815 this had been largely replaced by the village commune or *mir*. Most villages at the time were made up of a number of smaller extended families and had less than 500 inhabitants. Decision-making, binding on the whole village, was carried out by a group made up of the heads of families. This appears to have suited the landlords, the peasants and the circumstances of the time. Landlords found it easier to deal with one representative of an extended family, rather than the individual members. The *mir* council also acted as a self-regulating body, which took the administrative burden away from the landlord, dealing with the vexed question of allotting land to members of the commune and administering taxes and rents. The *mir* also seems to have given the majority of peasants a feeling of security which they desired. The communal nature of the organisation suited the situation. The short growing season demanded bursts of intense, coordinated activity, while the shortage of fertile land made such cooperation and coordination even more important.

  ★ There were two main categories of peasant: the serfs, who were privately owned; and the state peasants who lived on land which had not been given to private ownership and were therefore owned by the state. The serfs were the property of their owner and could be bought and sold, made to work where the owner wished and had virtually no effective legal rights. Although, along with the state peasants, their lives were often hard and unrewarding, comparisons with the slave plantations of America, or even the collective farms of Stalin's era, are misleading. As will be discussed later, there were many moral and economic arguments against the system, but the peasants were generally free to keep the profits of their labour, if they could make any, over and above the demands of their landlord or the state. These demands were growing as the landowning class increasingly fell into debt, but economic expediency, coupled with the inefficiency of the system, prevented the majority of landlords from placing impossible demands on their serfs. The peasants lived an alternately rigorous and monotonous life, but their existence was comparable to those of peasants in any pre-industrial society.

* The peasantry made up about 83 per cent of the population. What of the remainder? The most accurate figures for the period come from Arsenev, a statistician who produced the following table, which divided Russia's population into two groups – productive and unproductive. This table raises the importance at the time of various 'legal' definitions of class, which formed important barriers between the classes.

Arsenev's Table of Classes – Based on the censuses of 1812 and 1816

Unproductive Classes	Thousands	Percentage
Nobility	450	1.1
Clergy	430	1.1
Military	2,000	5.0
Officials (various types) and *Raznochintsy* (people of mixed ranks)	1,500	3.7
TOTAL	4,380	10.9
Productive Classes		
Merchants	204	0.5
Meschanin (shopkeepers and artisans)	1,490	3.7
State peasants	13,100	32.7
Serfs	20,300	50.7
'Free people' (mainly Cossacks)	234	0.6
Other peasants	360	0.9
TOTAL	35,688	99.1
Total	40,068	100.0

The most important aspect of this table is that it shows that there was a very small 'middle class'. The 'middle class' which did exist was strictly controlled. *Meshchanin* was a legal term which covered a variety of the poorer town-dwellers such as labourers, artisans and small shopkeepers. They could engage in business, but only within strictly defined limits on what and how much they could buy and sell. If they were particularly successful, they could try to join one of the merchant guilds. This involved the payment of an entry fee as well as a legal change of status. Even when the money for this could be raised, the authorities frequently did not allow this change of status to take place. Even if they gained the rights of a merchant, they still had to work within the strict rules laid down by the state for the guild they joined. Movement between classes was difficult at any level, but as a rule the lower down the scale you were, the more difficult it was. However, even serfs were theoretically able to, and sometimes did, buy their freedom.

The *Raznochintsy* were a mixed group. They were relatively well-educated people, but because they were not nobles, and were only of low 'rank', they did not easily fit into normal classifications. They were important for two main reasons. They were to provide the basis of the Russian intelligentsia, which in turn provided many of the leaders of the Russian revolutionary movements. They also brought to the fore the problems of the system of 'ranks'. The 'Table of Ranks' was inextricably linked to the nature and form of the Russian autocracy. It demonstrated and characterised the hierarchical nature of Russian society. Everyone had a place and station in life, and it was very difficult to alter that place and station. This naturally tended to stifle ambition, enterprise and initiative.

3 The Autocracy

Autocracy in Russia was autocracy in perhaps its purest form. All policy and decision-making lay in the hands of the Tsar. The Tsar expected, and for the most part received, the willing and total submission of his subjects. All his subjects were theoretically equal before him. His task was to be the strong 'father' who loved all his 'children' equally, who punished them when necessary, who kept order and who protected the fatherland from external threat. In his turn, he was subject to and responsible to God, and was held to be responsible for the spiritual and physical well-being of his people.

Some may feel that distinct similarities and parallels exist between this type of ruler and the 'Divine Right' monarchs of western Europe. However, this is a misleading comparison, with the possible exception of Spain in an earlier period. In Russia the autocrat had virtually never shared power with other groups. The great majority of Russians believed this was as it should be. They felt that the sharing of power would lead to corruption and the growth of privileged groups. They regarded the idea of privilege as inherently evil, something which would lead to weakness and misery for all. Until as recently as the later nineteenth century, many strong critics of the regime did not question the *idea* of autocracy, but rather focused on corrupt or inefficient officials or landlords. Even the serfs tended to see the Tsar as their 'little father' who was merely misled by his advisers.

* Why was the autocracy seen in this light? The reason lies partly in

the size, nature and scope of the Russian Empire. The task of ruling and defending such a vast and sprawling country, which possessed no effective natural defences, was not an easy one. It was made up of numerous nationalities, such as the Ukrainians and Lithuanians in the west, the Georgians and Cossacks in the south, and the Uzbeks and Tartars in the east. Russia needed strong government. The danger of invasion seemed always to be present. Also the Tsar's armies had been responsible for Russia's expansion and were therefore seen as closely linked to Russia's power and prestige. At the same time, Russian government required a complex hierarchy. The land was divided into

'Between Europe and Asia' – medieval Russian map

provinces which were sub-divided into districts, and further divided down to the village. This was because communications were so slow that the vast distances involved required the Tsar's representatives in the far-flung outposts of the Empire, at whatever level, to wield power for him. This had two major effects. Firstly it made the Tsar remote from his people, and often led them to blame his representatives for their problems rather than the Tsar. Secondly, the very complexity of the hierarchy acted as a brake on innovation and progress. The Orthodox Church, which saw the Tsar as an emperor (*autokrator*), also played a major part. It was, to a large extent, an unworldly Church. Its main emphasis was on ritual and the next world as opposed to the passing vagaries of this world. But it actively supported a succession of Tsars as the rightful rulers of the country and thus provided a firm theological basis for the Tsarist autocracy. So, whilst the Orthodox Church did not take an active part in political affairs (largely because it did not see this world as being of great importance), it did have a major impact on how the Tsars were seen by the Russian people. If religion ever was the 'opium of the people', it was so in Russia more than in any other country.

   * The bureaucratic nature of Russian society had been formally categorised by Peter the Great in 1722 when he published the 'Table of Ranks'. This was part of his plan for restructuring the Russian state. The table divided the ruling class into 14 ranks. Each member of the nobility had to serve the Tsar for his whole life, either in military or civil service. In theory at least, each noble had to start at the lowest rank and work his way up the ladder. The top eight ranks brought hereditary nobility, whilst the lowest six ranks brought personal nobility. Nobles owed their position to their service to the Tsar. This was the opposite of the old *Boyar* (the traditional Russian noble) idea of inherent nobility. The original system of ranks set up by Peter the Great depended on lifelong service and the idea of promotion on merit.

   However, by 1815 promotion was already more often determined by length of service than by ability, and lifelong service was no longer compulsory. Without these elements, the system of ranks ceased to be a positive factor and instead became a stultifying force which militated against change, initiative and efficiency.

The 'Table of Ranks'

Rank	Military	Civil
1	Field Marshal	Chancellor
2	General	Active Privy Councillor
3	Lieutenant General	Procurator General
4	Major General	Privy Councillor
5	Brigadier	Civil Councillor
6	Colonel	Superior Court President
7	Lieutenant Colonel	Aulic Councillor

8	Captain	Collegial Assessor
9	First Lieutenant	Titular Councillor
10	Second Lieutenant	College Secretary
11	—	Ship's Secretary
12	Sub-Lieutenant	Provincial Secretary
13	Ensign 1st Class	Senate Registrar
14	Ensign 2nd Class	College Registrar

Many of the terms used above will be unfamiliar. A detailed knowledge of what they mean is not needed to see just how stratified the 'Table' was, and how easily such a system could become a negative force once the basis of promotion ceased to be merit and ability and became replaced by influence and length of service.

4   Trade, Industry and the Economy

The Russian economy is often dismissed as backward and under-developed at this time. This is a dangerous over-simplification. The Russian economy was neither static nor insignificant. It was developing, although at a much slower rate than economies in most other parts of Europe.

At the beginning of the nineteenth century, Russian iron smelting accounted for one third of the world's iron production and Russia exported over 50,000 tons a year, mainly to England. Iron production grew by over 50 per cent in the first half of the nineteenth century. This might appear to be an impressive rate of growth, but it was not. In 1800 Russian iron production was roughly the equivalent of English iron production. By 1850, England produced twelve times as much iron as Russia. This relative stagnation was the result of Russian iron becoming too expensive to sell in European markets. It was expensive partly because of the very high cost of transporting it from the distant Urals (the centre of the Russian iron industry), and partly because investment and modernisation did not take place in Russia as it did elsewhere. This was to some extent due to the government's policy of protecting Russian industry from foreign competition. Protection, coupled with the use of serf labour, meant that Russian industrialists did not perceive the need to institute significant change. The obvious economic benefits of change, present elsewhere in Europe, were lacking. Similarly, many of the factors normally seen as necessary for rapid industrial expansion – available capital, administrative flexibility and an established entrepreneurial class – were conspicuous by their absence. The woollen, coal and chemical industries suffered similar relative stagnation.

There was one area of significant progress during the first half of the nineteenth century. This was the cotton industry, which developed rapidly, using technology brought from England. The Russian cotton industry was able to expand firstly because the Napoleonic wars protected the home industry from English competition, which was then further protected by high tariffs after 1822. Secondly, after 1815, it was able to buy cheap yarn and later cheap spinning machines from England, because it suited the English to allow them to do so. Finally it benefited from being a new industry, which therefore suffered less from traditional restrictions. By 1850, the Russian cotton industry had become the fifth largest in the world. Even then, however, total production was not much above ten per cent of English production.

Nevertheless, it must be remembered that the lack of growth in the Russian economy was relative and not absolute. As an examination of the figures given below will show, there was real progress in absolute terms. It was only in relation to other, far more active economies, that Russia was stagnating.

The nature of the Russian state was largely responsible for this relative stagnation. Trade and industry took place in the traditional way, largely by means of the royal appointment of monopolies. A competitive business economy had not yet developed in Russia. The majority of domestic trade was carried out through the antiquated system of fairs, which were still responsible for the majority of internal trade until the 1860s. Both the state and private banking systems were weak and unstable, and money was scarce and subject to severe fluctuations in value. It was still very difficult to invest in companies and therefore to find capital for expansion and development. Joint stock companies only began to appear at the beginning of the nineteenth century, and even then they were severely restricted by state legislation until the latter half of the century. Thus the atmosphere, the freedom and the infrastructure which encouraged rapid economic growth in western Europe and America simply did not exist in Russia at this time.

Production figures

Product	Year	Total production in roubles
Cotton	1814	32,000
	1852	1,835,000
Wool	1815	785,000
	1852	29,077,000

Total exports rose on average by a factor of 10, in the period 1802–60.

Exports by value (in roubles)

Product	1802	1860
Wheat	1,158,000	37,508,000
Rye	1,600,000	12,117,000
Fat & Lard	2,752,000	18,221,000
Furs	720,000	2,394,000
Wool	275,000	19,748,000
Metals and metal products	1,370,000	2,569,000

Divisions in society

Social		Economic	
Nobility	1.1%	Unproductive	10.9%
Peasants and serfs	83.4%	Productive	89.1%
All other groups	15.5%		

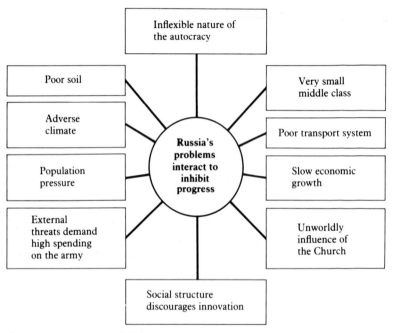

Summary – Russia in 1815

Making notes on 'Russia in 1815'

Your notes on this chapter should concentrate on the aspects which made Russia different from her European contemporaries. These are of central importance in understanding what took place in Russia in the nineteenth century. They not only set the scene, they also point towards the problems which Russia was to face and help to explain the limiting factors which the Tsars had to contend with.

The following headings should help you to make the very brief notes that you will require:

1.   Russian Geography
1.1. Vegetation; soil type; climate
1.2. Resulting problems

2.   Social Structure
2.1. Rural Russia
2.2. State peasants and serfs
2.3. 'Class' in Russia: nature and importance
3.   The Autocracy
3.1. Nature of the autocracy
3.2. Justifications of autocracy
3.3. The 'Table of Ranks'
4.   Trade, Industry and the Economy
4.1. Stagnation, progress, or both?

Source-based questions on 'Russia in 1815'

1   Russian Geography
Carefully study the map on page 2, the map on page 4 and the population graph on page 5. Then answer the following questions:
a)   What does the first map show about the relationship in size and geography between Russia and Europe? (2 marks)
b)   Why is the perspective so different from what you are used to? Does this mean that it is misleading? (5 marks)
c)   What implications did the situation portrayed in the population graph have for Russian agriculture and administration in the nineteenth century? (5 marks)
d)   What problems does the second map suggest this rise in population will cause? (3 marks)

2   The Economy
Carefully study the production and export figures given on page 11. Then:
a)   Draw a rough graph to show the percentage increase in cotton, iron and wool production. (7 marks)
b)   Describe what these graphs indicate about the comparative rate of growth of these industries. (3 marks)
c)   Explain what these figures might suggest about the growth of the Russian machine industry. (3 marks)
d)   Do the export and production figures give different pictures of the Russian economy? Explain any differences you find. (6 marks)

CHAPTER 2

Alexander I 1801–25

1 Alexander the Man

Alexander was something of an enigma. He has been seen by his critics as secretive, introspective, hypocritical and deceitful. His reign has often been characterised as a period of liberal intent followed by a period of severe repression. Whilst these comments contain an element of truth, they show only one side of the complex nature of both the man and his reign.

Alexander was born in 1777. He was the eldest son of the heir to the throne, Paul. He was taken from his parents by his grandmother the Empress Catherine. She took charge of his education and was determined that he should be groomed to be the ideal ruler of the future. She picked his tutors herself and personally wrote a number of texts for her grandson to study. Surprisingly, the most prominent of his tutors, La Harpe, was a Swiss and was both a republican and a democrat. La Harpe was Alexander's main intellectual guide from the age of seven to seventeen. A close bond grew up between tutor and student, and Alexander was certainly imbued at this early age with a respect and admiration for the ideas of liberty and equality which his tutor held.

When he was with his father, Alexander was exposed to a completely different regime. His father spent most of his time at his isolated residence of Gatchina, where he occupied himself by repeatedly drilling his small honour guard. Paul encouraged Alexander to become the perfect modern soldier, which for Paul meant strict discipline and regimentation on the Prussian model. Although this was something of a contrast to the spoiled existence Alexander enjoyed at his grandmother's court, he did seem to develop a real liking for the precision and order he found at Gatchina. However, relations between father and son were far from easy, and it is hardly surprising that the young Alexander became somewhat introspective and secretive, given the stark contrasts to which he was exposed.

Catherine died in 1796 and Paul came to the throne. In 1801 a group of officers planned to remove Paul, whom they rightly saw as unpredictable and ineffectual, and to place Alexander on the throne. They told Alexander of their plan, and he acquiesced on the condition that they would spare his father's life. They agreed to these conditions, and then, predictably perhaps, murdered Paul anyway. This involvement in his father's murder, although unintentional, led to feelings of guilt on Alexander's part which were to have a profound effect on him, particularly in later years.

2 The Early Years 1801–15

Alexander's reign is often divided into two – the period up to Napoleon's final defeat in 1815, and the period up to Alexander's death in 1825. Though such a division can be misleading, as will be seen below, it does have some merit.

Alexander's reign began with a distinctly liberal flourish. 1801 saw the repeal of almost all the harsh and oppressive legislation passed by Paul. Those who had been arrested were freed, those who had been exiled were allowed to return, and the use of torture was forbidden. Alexander wished that 'the very name of torture, the shame and reproach of humanity, will be wiped forever from the memory of the nation'. He attempted to establish a clear and fair legal system to replace the chaos of the existing one. Unfortunately, however, the commission which he set up to codify the law did not possess the necessary vision or strength to overcome the problems it faced. The new Tsar surrounded himself with young and forward-looking advisers. This group was known by its supporters as 'the committee of public salvation', and by its critics as the 'Jacobin Gang'. Both descriptions were somewhat wide of the mark, but they point clearly to the sharp division which existed between the liberal and conservative elements in Russian society.

Whatever Alexander's faults, significant legislation was passed during this period. The right to own estates was extended to 'free Russians' other than the nobility. In 1803 a law was enacted which allowed for voluntary emancipation of serfs by their masters. Although this measure has frequently been criticised because it did not go far enough, it was a significant measure and by 1850 over 100,000 male serfs had been emancipated with their families under the terms of this legislation. Improving the education system was made a priority. Several new universities were founded, along with over 40 secondary schools and numerous other schools.

The most comprehensive proposal for reform was drawn up by Speransky at Alexander's request. This was the plan for constitutional reform, which was completed in 1809. This plan envisaged three branches of government: legislature; executive and judiciary. The property-owning classes were to enjoy both civil and political rights, whilst the 'working people' were to enjoy civil rights. Alexander approved this plan in principle. It fitted in with his desire, expressed before his accession, 'to give Russia freedom and so save her from the encroachments of despotism and tyranny'. As a first step, in 1810, the Council of State was created to advise the Tsar. In an attempt to improve the vague and muddled nature of central government, new ministries were established with specific responsibilities. Clear guidelines were also set out on how they should carry out their duties. Some attempt was made to ensure that promotion in the civil service was once more by merit, rather than by seniority, with the introduction of examinations and qualifications.

* These changes were largely organised by Speransky. However, they provoked such strong opposition that Alexander was forced to dismiss him in March 1812. This dismissal illustrates the difference between theory and practice which characterised so much of Alexander's reign. The Tsar may have ruled supreme, but he still depended on the support of the nobility. The conservative élites in Russia may have shown no real sign of wishing to take power to themselves, but they certainly did not wish to give power to others, or to diminish their own importance. Alexander may have been able to take the almost revolutionary step of personally ordering that the treatise of the English reformer, Jeremy Bentham, on civil and penal law be translated into Russian, but he could not escape from the fact that he was the Tsar of a country whose people in practice had no civil rights as Bentham conceived them. As Tsar he was entrusted with the welfare of all his people, yet his actions were limited by the power structures of the Russian state and the need to maintain its stability, especially when Russia was threatened from abroad. Shortly after Speransky's dismissal, as the Tsar had expected, the alliance with France (at the Peace of Tilsit in 1807) broke down and Napoleon invaded. Russia needed unity to face this major threat. Other considerations had to be put aside, especially such potentially divisive ones as the need for reform. For the next three years Alexander concentrated on the defeat of Napoleon and the peace negotiations which followed.

* Alexander played a major part in bringing about Napoleon's defeat. He was hailed as the 'hero of liberation', a role which he felt to be justly his. He insisted on taking a personal role in the post-Napoleonic settlement. There seems little doubt that he felt that he had some form of divine mission to accomplish. At the time this mission was apparently quite liberal. He insisted that the restored French monarchy grant a constitution to its people. Although some doubted his motives, he insisted on the formation of a Polish state, with himself at its head. He granted the new state a constitution which many contemporaries thought remarkably liberal, in that it granted civil rights in Poland, which were not granted in Russia. The religious element came to the fore in the Holy Alliance (see page 107), which embodied Alexander's own personal vision for the future. It exhorted his fellow Christian monarchs to live as brothers and to preserve peace as a holy duty, according to the 'supreme truths dictated by the eternal law of God the Saviour'. Though England refrained from joining the alliance and the British Foreign Minister, Castlereagh, went so far as to call the whole enterprise 'a piece of sublime mysticism and nonsense', all the other Christian heads of state in Europe, with the exception of the Pope, joined the alliance. Yet it was only Alexander who really seems to have viewed this alliance as part of a 'Holy mission' to carry out God's will on earth.

3 Alexander After 1815

The period after 1815 is often seen as a period of reaction in Russia, in which the Tsar steadily moved away from his early liberal ideas towards a period of brutal repression. This view has some basis in terms of what actually took place, but it is a misrepresentation of Alexander's intent. Perhaps the best summation of Alexander's character comes from the acute observations of Prince Metternich:

> 1 The Emperor seized an idea, and followed it out quickly. It grew in his mind for about two years, till it came to be regarded by him as a system. In the course of the third year he remained faithful to the system he had adopted and learned to love, listened with real
> 5 fervour to its promoters, and was inaccessible to any calculation as to its worth or dangerous consequences. In the fourth year the sight of these consequences began to calm down his fervour; the fifth year showed an unseemly mixture of the old and nearly extinct system with the new idea. This new idea was often
> 10 diametrically opposed to the one he had just left.

However, despite this judgement Metternich saw that Alexander's 'disposition was noble, and his word was sacred'.

Alexander's underlying aims did not change during this period. He wanted what was best for his people. What did change were the expectations of many Russians, and the policies which the Tsar felt to be in the best interests of the Russian state. It is not surprising that at the end of the War of Liberation many Russians believed that the Tsar, who had brought freedom to so much of Europe and expounded so many forward-looking ideas, would come home to bring similar benefits to his own people. Alexander did intend to bring benefits to the Russian people, but not in the way his more liberal contemporaries hoped. He now saw his 'duty' as extending beyond Russia's frontiers to the rest of Europe. If he was to play a leading role in international affairs, as he was determined to do, he had to ensure that Russia maintained her pre-eminent position amongst the European powers.

* The first major reform Alexander embarked on was the expansion of the system of Military Colonies, which thus far had been limited to one small experiment. The Military Colonies were set up by ordering all the men from a particular regiment to report to a chosen area with their families. When they arrived they would work with the existing peasants to clear away all the old buildings and to create a completely new settlement. This was constructed according to clear, modern and

well-thought out plans supplied by the Special Corps of Military Colonies. The soldiers, their families, the existing peasants and the future children of all became subject to the strict regimentation of these colonies for life. All members of the colony were subject to the control of specially appointed officers. They were told when to work and at what. They were told whom to marry and when, and even how many children to have. The initial quota was set at one child per year per couple. Married women deemed capable of having children were fined if they did not produce children on schedule. Alexander hoped in one move to improve the situation of a significant number of peasants and their families, and to improve the nature and efficiency of Russia's standing army. This laudable aim did partially succeed in its intention, and at first was welcomed by many liberals as a move away from serfdom, but it soon became the focus for the most severe criticism of the Tsar.

Over a quarter of the standing army became colonists. The colonies, some of which were maintained up to 1857, did bring material benefits. They were far more efficient than the traditional estate. Living conditions, especially housing, food, clothing and security, were well above the norm for the period. However, this did not mean that they were particularly well-received by the participants. Soldiers who had become accustomed to military life did not react well to suddenly finding themselves in full uniform behind an ox-drawn plough. Sporadic revolts took place which were met with speedy and traditionally brutal punishment. The peasants found themselves subject to the same harsh regime. Whole villages begged to be exempted from becoming members of the colonies and losing what they saw as their traditional freedom. At best they proved reluctant converts to their new way of life. Vigel, a contemporary critic, summed up the shortcomings of the Military Colonies:

> 1 . . . two conflicting vocations were joined in one yoke; the farmer was made to take up the gun and the soldier the plough; the poor colonists were condemned to perpetual forced labour . . . Everything was in the Prussian manner, everything was subject to
> 5 accounting, everything was by weight and measure. Exhausted by labour in the fields, the Military Colonists were formed into ranks and drilled.

* The reluctance of the colonists was increased by the very strict discipline they faced. This was largely due to General Arakcheyev's control of the colonies. Arakcheyev was noted as a strict and brutal disciplinarian in an age when strict discipline was the norm. He became the focal point for liberal grievances. As Alexander increasingly left the day-to-day administration of the Empire to him, Arakcheyev's own particular, ruthlessly efficient, but soulless brand of administration grew steadily more prevalent throughout the Empire. Alexander's attitude to such harsh discipline seems to have been that it was a regrettable necessity. After Arakcheyev had put down one revolt in the Military Colonies, he wrote to Alexander describing how he was torn between his feelings as a Christian and the need to act decisively. He decided on sending the offenders twelve times through a gauntlet of 1000 men, each man administering one blow to the offender on each run through the gauntlet. This was a common form of punishment, except for the fact that once through the gauntlet was more normal. Twenty-five of the offenders died, not unnaturally as each of them should have received 12,000 blows. Alexander replied, 'I know exactly how your sensitive soul must have suffered in these circumstances'.

   * The second major area of reform which Alexander promoted was in the field of education. He felt that the education system was inefficient and lacked the necessary rigour to produce men of the calibre needed by the army and the civil service. Alexander was increasingly preoccupied by his feeling of being a chosen agent of God's will. Therefore, he felt that the person to oversee this reform should be a man of deep religious conviction. He chose Prince Golitsyn, who had long been his friend and who had been partly responsible for his growing personal interest in religion.

   Golitsyn had been Over Procurator of the Holy Synod since 1803. This was a very influential government post, which entailed overseeing the activities of the Orthodox Church. He was also head of the Russian Bible Society, which had recently been formed with the intention of translating the Bible into Russian. Now, in 1817, he became head of the new Ministry of Spiritual Affairs and Education. He believed in the Scriptures as the basis of all truth. With these credentials, one might have expected him to be the arch traditionalist. This he most certainly was not. He was a man of remarkable toleration for the time, despite the fact that he expelled the Jesuits. He naturally had a leaning towards the Orthodox Church, but he also expressed interest in, and a friendly disposition towards, Catholics, Lutherans and even the Quakers. This did not please the Orthodox bishops.

   Golitsyn's main aim was for as many people as possible to read the Bible so that they could discover divine truth for themselves. He believed the Scriptures would provide the only effective antidote to freethinking rationalism, which he saw as being a major cause of the problems which faced Russian and indeed European society at the time. This 'freethinking' was at the heart of the 'Enlightenment' of the previous century and involved questioning all existing social and political structures.

   The guiding tenet of the new ministry was laid down by Alexander at its inception. He stated that he expected that from that point 'Christian piety would be the basis of all true education'. One presumes that as Alexander chose Golitsyn to head the new ministry, he expected this sentiment to be implemented with a degree of liberality. It seems that Golitsyn did have liberal aims, but he was not capable of maintaining a tight rein on such a vast enterprise. He was perhaps justly respected as a saintly individual of deep moral conviction, and was considered by many to be something of a mystic. But he was not an able enough administrator to control the hundreds of civil servants who would have to put his beliefs into practice, and who were in general decidedly less liberal than himself.

Within a short space of time the new ministry earned the nickname of 'Ministry of Darkness'. Those who administered policies tended to take the Tsar's statement at face value, in a narrow and very restrictive sense. Even conservative commentators felt that the new ministry went far beyond reasonable bounds. An often-quoted example was the banning by the censors of a book on poisonous mushrooms. They argued that as mushrooms formed the main food of the Orthodox during Lent, they were sacred, and that therefore to describe them as being poisonous was sacrilege. Both literature and the theatre also came under increasing scrutiny lest they exert a 'corrupting influence'.

The universities also suffered, Kazan being the clearest example. In 1819, Magnitsky, an officer in the Ministry of Education, was sent to inspect Kazan University. Magnitsky was an extreme example of the bigoted and narrow-minded Russian administrator. He found a hot-bed of radical 'freethinking', and recommended to the Tsar that the University be closed down immediately. Alexander was not prepared to go that far, but he made Magnitsky the head of the Kazan educational district, and gave him the task of purging the University of dangerous ideas and influences. Magnitsky set about the task with fervour. He dismissed the director and almost half the academic staff and replaced them with pious but ill-qualified substitutes. He removed hundreds of books which he considered suspect, including those of Newton and Copernicus. He imported Bibles by the case. He ordered that lecture notes be regularly examined, and employed people to listen closely to general student conversations to ensure that they did not contain any impious sentiments. Students who exhibited such tendencies were made to wear signs branding them 'sinner'. Serious offenders were put into solitary confinement, whilst the rest of the student body prayed for their salvation. Kazan was the oustanding case of such repression, but all the universities suffered similar interference to some degree, with the notable exception of Moscow, which escaped – perhaps due to the fact that it was the oldest and most respected of the universities.

Young liberals became increasingly frustrated with what they saw as a growing tide of repression. As one Guards officer, who had returned from France, later wrote:

1 Seeing the insipid life in St. Petersburg and listening to the babblings of old men praising the past and deprecating every

progressive step was unbearable. We were a hundred years from them.

In 1818 a number of these liberals formed a secret society called the 'Union of Welfare' to try to put their views into practice. Their feelings were heightened by the continued liberal stance of Alexander abroad. He encouraged constitutional development in Poland; he supported the granting of constitutions by the German princes and at first he appeared to support the nationalist revolt of the Greeks against the Turks; but he stood firmly against any such liberal moves at home.

However, it would be too simplistic to argue that Alexander was repressive at home and liberal abroad. In fact, Alexander had not yet become a reactionary. It was just that by concentrating on affairs abroad, he allowed reactionary elements at home to dominate. Between 1816 and 1820, he spent two thirds of his time out of the country. He left the running of the Empire largely in the hands of Golitsyn and Arakcheyev. The former was incapable of controlling the reactionary inclinations of his subordinates, whilst the latter was a bureaucrat by nature who believed that opposition needed to be dealt with ruthlessly. The Tsar had not lost his liberal tendencies: he felt rather that he had found a higher purpose. What he thought of as a God-given mission to serve the greater good of mankind now occupied him more than domestic considerations.

Yet Alexander had not completely forgotten Russia. In 1819, Speransky was appointed as Governor of Siberia and was given the task of reforming the administration. In 1818, Alexander had asked Novosiltsev to draw up a constitution. Novosiltsev based his draft constitution largely on the Polish model. The Tsar was to remain the sole source of authority in the Empire, but 'the representative assembly of the state' was to assist the sovereign. Regional assemblies were to discuss local affairs and to nominate members of the national assembly. The draft also guaranteed basic civil liberties. Novosiltsev presented it to Alexander early in 1820. Today the draft does not appear particularly liberal. For example, the national assembly was only to meet every five years. Nonetheless, it would have been a major step forward for Russia, and might have provided the basis for future constitutional developments. It was certainly considered sufficiently revolutionary by Nicholas I eleven years later for him to order all printed copies to be burned. There is no reason to suppose that the Tsar might not have attempted to implement the charter had other events not intervened.

* 1820 seems to mark the real end of Alexander's struggle to remain a liberal autocrat. He believed that events threatened both the international order and the order within his own empire. Successive revolutions in Spain, Naples and Portugal forced the granting of constitutions or brought constitutional monarchs to the throne. Alexander believed that there was an international conspiracy against Christianity and monarchy, founded on the 'so-called philosophy of Voltaire and his like'. He urged strong and vigorous action against the revolutionaries. This was very much an about-face for the former pupil of La Harpe. He recognised this quite clearly in a statement to Metternich:

1 From 1813 to 1820 is seven years, and these seven years are like a century to me. In 1820 I will at no price do what I did in 1813. You are not altered but I am. You have nothing to regret, but I have.

Alexander was thinking here about international events. However, news brought to him at the Congress of Troppau (see page 109) in November 1820 turned his attention back to domestic affairs. The Semyonovsky Guards, one of the Tsar's own élite and favourite regiments, had mutinied in St Petersburg. Alexander would not have been unduly surprised at the news of a small peasant revolt. Indeed throughout the previous year there had been continuing unrest in the Cossack region. Nor would he have been more than displeased and perhaps disappointed to hear of further unrest in the Military Colonies. But mutiny in one of his own élite regiments was almost beyond his comprehension. The revolt itself did not involve violence or bloodshed. The Guards had complained about their treatment and had refused to disperse when ordered to do so. However, having made their protest, they had quietly accepted arrest. Such action still constituted mutiny and was almost without precedent. The subsequent report from St Petersburg laid the blame for the revolt squarely upon the new commander, Colonel Schwarz. He had introduced a degree of rigid discipline which went far beyond normal standards, even in those rigorous times. The report naturally recommended firm punishment, but did not ascribe political motives to the revolt.

However, Alexander felt that this was another example of the 'international conspiracy'. He could not believe that the men could have mutinied without the encouragement of their officers. He felt that the officers must have wished to distract him from his task of quelling revolution abroad. Arakcheyev's power and influence grew and repression became the norm. The role of the secret police was expanded and censorship became progressively tighter under their influence. In the end even Golitsyn fell from grace because he offended the censor. This is perhaps not surprising since he authorised the publication of a work, prepared by the Bible Society, which suggested that the Virgin Mary had given birth to sons fathered by Joseph. The Orthodox Church viewed such a suggestion as blasphemy and yet another example of dangerous freethinking. Censorship became so strict that an anonymous article by Magnitsky, which strongly attacked the whole idea of constitutions, was rejected on the grounds that no comment needed to be made on constitutions. If any comment were needed the government would provide it. In such a climate, Golitsyn had gone too far and the Tsar dismissed him from his post. Shishkov replaced him as Minister of Education. Shishkov was an ageing reactionary, well-known for his view that education was dangerous and subversive in anything more than very small doses. He was an ideally safe candidate for the Ministry of Education.

* The Union of Welfare was not inactive during this period of growing repression. In 1821, its leaders examined their position carefully. They feared, rightly, that they might have been infiltrated by informers. They therefore disbanded with the intention of re-forming almost immediately, taking far greater care over whom they admitted to their ranks. The ploy worked. An official report was sent to Alexander stating that the Union, which he had not even heard of up to this point, had existed but had now broken up. The Union developed into two secret organisations which were geographically based, the Northern Society and the Southern Society. Both grew rapidly. Most new members were young officers. They were inspired by their experience abroad and by the example of the few Spanish officers who had obtained a constitution for their country by leading a revolt there in 1820. They were embittered by what they saw at home. The Southern Society, led by Paul Pestel, was always the better organised and the more active, but the Northern Society also became increasingly of the view that direct action might be needed. By 1825, they had decided that they needed to take drastic action. They would be ready to assassinate Alexander in the summer of 1826. They were convinced that the officers involved in the two societies would easily be able to persuade their men to follow them, and that they would be able to set up a provisional assembly after the assassination. However, their plans lacked firm detail. As yet they had not even agreed on what type of constitutional government they sought. Their plans were so imprecise that they may well have come to nothing had not Alexander precipitated a crisis both by his death and by the fact that he had not made public the arrangements for his succession.

In 1822, Alexander had persuaded the Grand Duke Constantine, his elder brother and next in line of succession, to renounce his claim to the throne. Alexander did this because Constantine had no children to continue the dynasty, and because, since Constantine's remarriage to a non-royal Polish Countess, any future children he might have would not be able to come to the Russian throne legally.

Constantine readily agreed to this and confirmed his agreement in writing. Alexander then issued a secret decree naming his younger brother Nicholas, who did have a son, as his heir. He told only a few close advisers of this arrangement. Even Nicholas did not know of it! We do not know exactly why he took this course of action, but it seems likely that it was because he found the throne such a burden himself. He apparently did not wish to interrupt the relatively carefree life

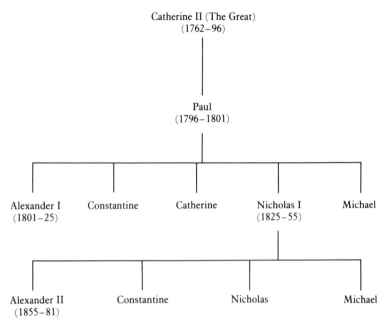

Catherine II (The Great)
(1762–96)

Paul
(1796–1801)

Alexander I (1801–25) — Constantine — Catherine — Nicholas I (1825–55) — Michael

Alexander II (1855–81) — Constantine — Nicholas — Michael

The Romanovs – Catherine the Great to Alexander II

which Nicholas enjoyed by laying this burden upon him.

Alexander's last months saw him apparently losing touch with reality. His wife was ill and he seems to have been preoccupied with her health and in making amends to her for his well-known relationship with his mistress. He decided to spend the winter in the southern town of Tagnarog, which was unpopular both because of its climate and its isolation. After he left St Petersburg he received a letter from Arakcheyev, stating that he had had to abandon his duties and retire to his estates in mourning. His notoriously cruel mistress, Nastasya Minkin, had provoked her serfs once too often and had been murdered by them. Shortly afterwards Alexander received a report about the activities of the Southern Society, which contained enough detail to mention Pestel by name. Perhaps because he had no Arakcheyev to consult, the Tsar decided against taking any immediate action. He went on a short tour of the Crimea, where he fell ill. Returning to Tagnarog, he died a fortnight later on 19 November 1825, after a brief illness.

There has been much controversy over Alexander's death. Persistent rumours held that he did not die, but faked his death so that he could slip into obscurity as a wandering mystic. These rumours were encouraged by three main factors: the strange choice of the isolated Tagnarog as a place to spend the winter; the fact that early in his reign he had stated his wish to lay aside the responsibility of office as soon as was practicable; and later by the fact that when his coffin was opened by Alexander III, it was found to be empty. It is unlikely that these rumours will ever be conclusively proved or disproved. What is certain, however, is that in November 1825, Alexander ceased to be Tsar of Russia. What is also certain is that he contributed to the confusion after his death, by not taking decisive action against the Southern Society and by not clearly settling the matter of his succession. This inaction was a significant factor in bringing about the Decembrist Revolt (see page 30).

4   Assessment

In terms of what actually took place, one may divide Alexander's reign in two: a period of apparent liberalism followed by a period of reaction and repression. However, such a division gives the impression that Alexander was in full control of what took place and that he became reactionary. This impression is misleading. There was an almost inevitable dualism present throughout his reign. He wished to be a liberal autocrat! This meant that he had to balance the forces of change against the need to maintain the stability of the autocratic system, of which he was both figurehead and foundation. Even towards the very end of his reign, just before he left for Tagnarog and after the most active period of repression, he expressed the hope that he might be able to grant his people a constitution. This does not fit in with the picture of a reactionary monarch.

It may be that his official biographer, Schilder, writing at the end of the nineteenth century, was correct in describing Alexander as a spent force after 1815:

1 The whole store of Alexander's will power, seemed spent in his struggle with Napoleon, which placed the utmost strain on all his physical and spiritual strength, and it is not surprising that the Tsar displayed fatigue and mental exhaustion.

This would certainly be a very elegant explanation if it could be sustained. The problem with it is that after 1815, Alexander was remarkably active in the field of foreign affairs, displaying great tenacity and achieving significant success. Perhaps Speransky's judgement that Alexander was 'too weak to rule, too strong to let others rule' contains more truth. But 'too weak' in what sense? He was too weak to implement many of the reforms he wanted, in the way he wanted. The real question is, was he too weak because he lacked the nerve to force through his reforms, or because he was too busy with foreign affairs, or was it that he was unable to overcome the near-immobility of the Russian state? All three factors are important, but when faced by overwhelming conservative pressure, Alexander had to give way. In 1812 he dismissed Speransky, and in 1824 he dismissed Golitsyn. It may be that he lost heart somewhat in terms of domestic reform and was naturally enticed towards foreign affairs, where he seemed to be able to attain greater and more rapid success. However, he did not forget the idea of a constitution. In 1818 and in 1825 he expressed a clear desire to implement such a project. The surprising fact is not that he could not find a way of doing so, but rather that he seriously contemplated such a move at all. It seems that Alexander did sincerely wish to be a 'liberal autocrat'. Whilst it is true that he failed in the eyes of many contemporaries and more recent critics, it is also true that many of his contemporaries saw him as far too liberal. This view was certainly held by many of his fellow monarchs and the conservative élite in Russia itself. Metternich saw him as a dangerous 'son of the Enlightenment'. In some ways Alexander disappointed so many because he promised so much. He tried to be liberal, whilst remaining an autocrat in an autocratic country. Such a course was never likely to be an easy one to follow.

Making notes on Alexander I 1801–25

Your notes should bring out the dual nature of Alexander's rule. He sought to be a liberal autocrat, which is a contradiction in terms. Therefore you must be aware of how these contradictions affected his actions. You also need to bring out the ways in which the conservative forces in Russia reacted against reform, and how they often altered the actual impact of reform, particularly in the case of the military and education. The difference between intended outcome and actual outcome is very important.

The following headings should help you to include the key points:

1.   Alexander the Man
2.   The Early Years
2.1. Early reform
2.2. Restraints on reform
2.3. Preoccupation abroad
3.   After 1815
3.1. Changing expectations
3.2. The Military Colonies
3.3. Education, Golitsyn and reform?
3.4. Positive moves for reform
3.6. Repression
3.7. Revolutionary plans and Alexander's death
4.   Assessment

1801	Liberal reform	1811

Exiles allowed to return to Russia	Serfs could be freed	Plan for constitutional reform	Council of state established

Repressive laws repealed	Torture forbidden	Reform of the civil service

1812

Speransky dismissed

Napoleon invades

1815

Alexander concentrates on Europe and the peace settlement

1816	Liberal and repressive?	1820

At home

Abroad

Establishes Military Colonies

Tighter control of education (apparent repression)

Speransky recalled

Draws up a constitution

Gives Liberal constitution to Poland

Gives liberal support to German states and Greece

1821	Repression abroad and at home	1825

Revolts put down at home and abroad	Censorship rigidly imposed	Golitsyn dismissed

Summary – Alexander I 1801–25

Answering essay questions on Alexander I 1801–25

The information in this chapter should enable you to answer general questions on Alexander I. These usually take the following form:

1. 'What were the main aims of Alexander I's domestic policies?'
2. 'How far did Alexander I's liberal education lead to liberal policies and achievements when he became Tsar?'
3. ' "Enigmatic" – how accurate a description of Alexander I's personality and policies is this?'

Question 1 appears to be a straightforward 'what' question. Make a list of the major reforms and initiatives put forward by Alexander. Then put them into a table with the following headings: *Reform or initiative*; *Motivation of*; *Reaction to*; *Defects of*. You should now see the hidden complexity of the question. One underlying aim of Alexander's reforms was to create a strong Russia. Most of his subjects shared that aim. The problem is that there were different views on how to achieve it. Alexander himself was always caught between the desire to reform and improve, and the desire to maintain power and stability. In particular the column marked 'Reaction to' should have raised the very important question of reaction from *whom?* Many reforms generated positive and negative reactions. Similarly the motivation behind Golitsyn's reforms was not shared by many who put them into practice. This becomes important when you consider that the majority of Alexander's later domestic policies were not actually his, but were the policies of those he put in power.

Bearing these issues in mind draw up an essay plan for question 1. Try to put Alexander's reforms into groups. You could try 'type of reform' and 'period of reform' to see which is most successful. When you have done this, decide which approach is most effective and why.

Questions 2 and 3 have a different emphasis, though they will make use of much the same information as question 1.

Source-based questions on Alexander I 1801–25

1   Alexander's Character
Read the description of Alexander given by Metternich on page 17, and answer the following questions:
a)   What opinion does Metternich have of Alexander? (5 marks)
b)   If this opinion was correct, what problems was it likely to cause the government of Russia? (5 marks)

c)   Metternich was an accurate and acute observer. He was also a very conservative politician who was responsible for Austrian foreign policy. How does this affect the weight we should place on this piece of evidence? (5 marks)

2   The Military Colonies

Carefully read the extract from Vigel on the Military Colonies given on page 20 and answer the following questions:
a)   What does Vigel mean by the 'Prussian manner'? (1 mark)
b)   In what ways and on what basis does this extract criticise the Military Colonies? (6 marks)
c)   Does the criticism offered suggest that Vigel was something of a 'romantic'? If so, how would this affect your view of his evidence? (3 marks)
d)   Was the negative reaction described by Vigel an 'inevitable' product of the formation of the Military Colonies? Explain your answer. (5 marks)

3   Alexander and Reform

Study the extract from the Guards officer on page 20 and the extract from Alexander on page 22. Answer the following questions:
a)   What mood is expressed in each extract? (4 marks)
b)   What different events have prompted these statements? (2 marks)
c)   What conclusions might each extract support? (6 marks)
d)   How might you try to check the validity of these extracts as evidence for your study of the period? (3 marks)

CHAPTER 3

Nicholas I 1825–55

1 The Decembrist Revolt

The Decembrist Revolt was prompted by three main factors. The failure of the authorities to take decisive action over the secret societies allowed the societies time to act. The confusion over the succession provided the opportunity for the societies to gain support from otherwise loyal elements in Russian society. And the justified fear of those societies that their plans had been discovered led to the date for the planned revolt being brought forward.

When news of Alexander's death arrived in St Petersburg, his secret manifesto was opened and Nicholas was told for the first time of his position. The evidence suggests that his first thought was to publish the manifesto and proclaim himself Tsar. But the Governor General of St Petersburg, Miloradovich, counselled a more cautious course of action. He reminded Nicholas that, according to custom, Constantine became Tsar immediately on Alexander's death. This, coupled with the fact that Nicholas was far from popular with the Guards, led the governor to suggest that Nicholas proclaim Constantine as Tsar, and then wait for Constantine to renounce the throne before proclaiming himself Tsar. Nicholas decided to follow this advice because he was not sure of the Guards' support. He knew that the Guards had intervened in the succession on a number of previous occasions. He therefore proclaimed Constantine as Tsar and sent a courier to Warsaw to inform his brother of what he had done.

The situation was complicated by the nature of communications in Russia. News of Alexander's death had reached Constantine in Warsaw two days before it reached Nicholas in St Petersburg. Constantine had proclaimed Nicholas as Tsar, and had written to Nicholas informing him of his action. Each brother had proclaimed the other as Tsar. Effective communications between the two were hampered by the fact that it took seven days for a message to travel from Warsaw to St Petersburg. The letters from the two brothers had therefore crossed. On receiving the first letter from Warsaw, Nicholas at once wrote again to Constantine asking him to return to the capital. This letter arrived in Warsaw on 2 December. Constantine sent back a peremptory reply stating that he would not come to St Petersburg as he could see no reason for doing so, and that he would be grateful if Nicholas would stop bothering him and got on with his duties as Tsar. Several equally fruitless communications followed, which did not affect Constantine's decision.

  * Whilst this ludicrous situation continued the secret societies were given a breathing space. They had intended to act the following

summer. It was now clear that they would have to bring their plans forward, especially as they rightly suspected that part of their plans had been made known to the authorities. The Southern Society was by far the better organised, but the Northern Society was centrally placed in the capital, St Petersburg. However, both groups were determined to act. Intense activity followed which tended to be long on rhetoric and very short on detailed planning. The officers involved seemed to have had a blind faith that their troops would follow them. They believed that the great majority of those who would not actively support them would at least not take direct action against them.

On Saturday 12 December, Nicholas received yet another letter from Constantine. He refused to come to the capital, but confirmed Nicholas as Tsar. Nicholas finally realised that Constantine would not come, and therefore made plans to publish the manifesto and to proclaim himself Tsar on Monday 14 December. On the same day, Nicholas also received reports giving specific details of the Southern Society and general details of the Northern Society. He was then informed by a Lieutenant Rostovstev of the plans of the Northern Society. There seems little doubt that had Arakcheyev been in place he would have taken decisive action. However, Miloradovich was apparently quite certain that the situation was under control. He assured Nicholas that the Northern Society's activities were being monitored, which was accurate, and that they posed no real threat, which was far from accurate. Nicholas decided to accept this reassurance, although he was apparently far from convinced. He did so on the grounds that he feared direct action against the conspirators might both provoke the revolt he sought to avoid, and persuade the Guards to support them.

Meanwhile, an extraordinary event occurred which perhaps gives an insight into the peculiar nature of Russian society at the time. Rostovstev, who had given the Tsar details of the Northern Society's activities, went from the Tsar to inform the Northern Society of his meeting with him. By his own lights he had therefore acted honourably. He had fulfilled his duty by keeping the Tsar informed of events. He had not actually betrayed his comrades by name to the Tsar, yet by keeping them appraised of events he preserved his own conscience. It seems that his aim was to prevent the revolt, without harming his comrades. Rostovstev's news naturally caused some consternation amongst the Society's members. The officers involved had planned to accuse Nicholas of seizing the throne from the legitimate ruler Constantine and thus convince their troops of the just nature of their cause. Some officers quietly withdrew from the scheme at this point, but others decided to continue with their plans.

* On the morning of Monday 14 December, the great majority of Guards calmly took their oath of allegiance. The rebels gathered in the Senate Square of St Petersburg, to demand that Constantine be maintained as Tsar. Miloradovich was still convinced that the matter

could be settled without resorting to force. He went alone to talk to the rebels and to explain their error to them. As he was about to leave, having failed to convince the rebels to go back to their barracks, he was shot by one of the more radical members of the group. He died later that day. Nicholas decided to take charge of the situation himself. The rebels had believed that certainly 8000, and possibly up to 20,000 troops would join them. In the event their numbers never rose above 3000. They were surrounded by some 10,000 loyal troops. Nicholas decided that a show of force would convince the rebels to retire. He ordered the cavalry to charge. What followed might have been funny, if the situation had not been so serious. The horses could not maintain a footing on the icy cobbles, and their charge was broken up by one volley from the rebels. For the next three hours the two forces faced each other, whilst Nicholas made repeated attempts to persuade the rebels to retire peacefully to their barracks. Nicholas wanted to avoid bloodshed which might arouse others and make the situation more dangerous. The rebels simply did not know what to do, except to wait and hope that others would rally to their banner. A few did so, but not enough to make any difference to the situation. As the light began to fail, after the rebels had been in the square for over five hours, Nicholas was finally persuaded to take firm action. He ordered the artillery to open fire. Within minutes the 'Decembrist Revolt' was at an end. The following is part of Nicholas's own account of that day:

1 ... I saw the regiment of Guards Grenadiers, in complete disorder, walking in a body with their colours but without officers. Suspecting nothing, I approached them, wanting to stop the men and place them in formation, but when I called out
5 'Halt!' they replied: 'We're for Constantine!'
   I indicated them Senate Square and said: 'In that case, that's your way.'
   And the entire throng walked past me, through all the troops, and joined without hindrance their equally misguided comrades.
10 This was fortunate, for otherwise bloodshed would have begun under the windows of the palace, and our fate would have been more than doubtful ...
   Then Adjutant General Vasil'chikov turned to me and said: 'Sire, there is not a moment to lose; there is nothing else to do
15 now. We must use grape-shot!' I had foreseen the necessity of this, but, I confess, when the time came, I could not make up my mind to such a measure. I was terror stricken. 'Do you wish me to spill the blood of my subjects on the first day of my reign?' I replied to Vasil'chikov. 'In order to save your reign' he answered
20 me.
   These words brought me back to myself; coming to my senses, I saw that I must either take it upon myself to spill the blood of a

few and almost surely save everything, or spare myself at the cost
of definitely sacrificing the state . . .

25   At that point, seeing no other alternative, I ordered: 'Fire!'

The revolt in the north was over. Thanks to firm action by the
authorities in the south, the much better organised revolt in that region
was also soon dealt with. However, the traumatic beginning to his reign
could not but affect the new Tsar.

* Historians have characterised the Decembrist Revolt in different
ways: as a traditional Russian aristocratic *coup*, and as a forerunner of
the popular movements which sought to remove the Tsarist autocracy.
There are elements of truth in both views. The Decembrists counted
amongst their number members of the country's most aristocratic
families. In many ways it was a traditional *coup* in that the great
majority of the Decembrists did not even contemplate involving the
mass of the people. They intended to rely on winning over substantial
elements of the army. However, they did wish to change the system.
Many of the officers involved had been inspired by what they had seen
in France at the end of the Napoleonic wars. Though there was no
overall agreement on what the changes should be, there was a general
agreement that change was necessary. Muraviev, the leader of the
Northern Society, wanted a federal system based on the American
model, with the Tsar effectively filling the position of President. Pestel,
the leader of the Southern Society, accepted regicide as a necessary evil
and sought to establish a republican system where 'all Russian citizens
should exercise equally all individual rights, civil and political', albeit
with those rights somewhat limited by a strong central government.
Whilst it is true that not all the conspirators fully shared the views of
either Pestel or Muraviev, these elements do make the Decembrist
Revolt something more than just another aristocratic *coup*. It may have
been traditional in form, but not in intent.

2   The Military Tsar

Nicholas has often been condemned as reactionary and unimaginative.
His reign began amidst the turmoil of the Decembrist Revolt, and
ended in the disaster of the Crimean War. Critics have argued that his
period as Tsar was characterised by repression and an absurd preoccupation with trivial detail. His supporters have pointed to a flowering
in the arts and to real progress in the realms of economic and technical
endeavour. His intentions were certainly not matched by results, but in
that he was far from being alone in terms of nineteenth-century Tsars.

Nicholas had not been brought up to be Tsar. He had sought nothing
more than to be an efficient, dedicated and effective officer. He had a
military respect for order, planning, uniformity and clearly defined
lines of responsibility. He did not wish to become Tsar, but once he

came to the throne he dedicated himself wholeheartedly to the task. Unlike Alexander he insisted on being in complete control of events within the Empire. He believed in firm, prompt action, and strict discipline. Above all he believed in the concept of duty to the fatherland, from the highest to the lowest. He applied strict standards to his own conduct and expected no less from his subordinates. One of the most perceptive analyses of Nicholas comes from Queen Victoria:

1 He is stern and severe – with fixed principles of duty which nothing on earth will make him change; very clever I do not think him, and his mind is an uncivilised one; his education has been neglected; politics and military concerns are the only things he
5 takes great interest in; the arts and all softer occupations he is insensible to, but he is sincere, I am certain, sincere even in his most despotic acts, from a sense that it is the only way to govern; he is not, I am sure aware of the dreadful cases of individual misery which he so often causes, for I can see by various instances
10 that he is kept in utter ignorance of many things, which his people carry out in most corrupt ways, while he thinks he is extremely just.

* Nicholas made an investigation of the nature and causes of the Decembrist Revolt his first priority. He was naturally alarmed by the revolt itself, but he was equally disturbed by the fact that the leaders of the revolt were for the most part representatives of Russia's oldest and most respected noble families. This investigation was to become the model for the future. It was extremely thorough and painstaking. It was carried out by a special committee appointed by Nicholas, which reported directly to him, and in whose proceedings he frequently took an active part. Nicholas was determined that the leaders should be firmly punished as an example to all that, no matter what a person's position in society, disloyalty would not be tolerated. In all over 3000 people were arrested. The majority of the rank and file soldiers were either severely reprimanded or subjected to the standard form of corporal punishment – running the gauntlet. Five of the leaders were sentenced to death and 116 were sentenced to exile in Siberia. This may not seem unduly harsh, but in Russia many contemporaries did think it so. This was partly because, technically, the death penalty was illegal in Russia. It had not been invoked since the Pugachev Rebellion, the great peasant revolt of 1775. There was also a long tradition of pardoning those who were exiled, for whatever reason, after a salutary period of isolation away from 'civilised' Russia. In the case of the Decembrists the five were hanged and those exiled were not allowed to return. In Nicholas's defence it should be noted that he commuted the sentence of the five from the barbarous 'quartering' (disembowellment), to hanging, and the sentence of 24 others from execution, to exile. However this did nothing to lessen the feeling that the sentences were unduly harsh.

* Nicholas was not only concerned with making an example of the leaders of the revolt – he also wished to deal with its causes. He wished to do so both in order to prevent a similar occurrence in the future, and to remedy the abuse and mismanagement which the committee had found to be so prevalent in Russian society. However, he did not accept that there was any fault in the idea of autocracy itself. The problems which were clearly detailed by the committee included: corruption and inefficiency in the administration; an antiquated legal system which had virtually broken down; a deterioration in the economic position of the nobility; and an increasing burden, in terms of both taxation and the need to increase productivity, on the peasant population. The committee produced a comprehensive report on the problems and grievances listed by the accused. Nicholas kept a personal copy of the report and determined to deal with many of the problems which it listed. He was also determined to limit the 'pernicious' spread of foreign ideas, which he felt must be responsible for the 'misguided' actions of the Decembrists.

Nicholas made a firm start to the task which he had set himself. The revolt and the report had left him with a mistrust of both the administration and the Russian nobility. He decided that he must keep personal control over the formation and implementation of future policy. This led him to form his own administration, the Imperial Chancery. He also surrounded himself with non-Russian advisers, in particular Benckendorf, Kankrin, Kiselev and Nesselrode. The Chancery had originally been organised to deal with matters which needed the Tsar's personal participation. Nicholas now felt that all aspects of the running of the Empire needed his personal consideration and the Chancery was expanded accordingly. This was not simply a move to take personal control, it was an attempt to bypass the inept bureaucracy of the established administration. The original Chancery became the First Section of His Majesty's Own Chancery, which functioned as his private secretariat. In 1826 he established the Second Section to deal with the codification of the Russian legal system. In the same year he established the Third Section, whose function was to monitor and regulate the activities of all 'suspicious and harmful people'. In 1828, the Fourth Section was set up to monitor and control the educational and charitable organisations which had previously been controlled by the Empress Dowager. Finally in 1836, a Fifth Section was formed to reorganise the administration of state peasants. This personal administration frequently bypassed normal channels. It gave the Tsar the ability to implement changes quickly, but led to a ridiculous situation in which some ministers did not know of major changes in their own areas, until they were actually decreed by the Tsar. It also led to the Tsar becoming increasingly overloaded with work.

Though Nicholas's treatment of the Decembrists was thought of as unduly severe by many people, some liberals did see reason for optimism. Nicholas's early dismissal of Arakcheyev and Magnitsky, the two members of Alexander's administration most closely associated with reaction, appeared to many liberal elements to bode well for the future. This feeling was reinforced by the appointment of Speransky to oversee the codification of the legal system by the Second Section. Nesselrode was maintained as Minister of Foreign Affairs, and Kankrin as Minister of Finance, but neither of these ministries were closely associated with the darker side of Alexander's reign. Nicholas stated clearly in his manifesto that change was needed, but he stated equally clearly his view on who should guide that change:

1 It is not by means of insolent and impractical projects, which are destructive, but it is from above, that national institutions are gradually improved, defects remedied, and abuses reformed.

3   The Chancery, Planning and Progress

Under Speransky, the Second Section set about its massive task with great speed and vigour. The Russian legal system was in chaos. The most recent code had been produced in 1649. Since then hundreds of laws had fallen into disuse, and hundreds of contradictory laws had been passed. Successive Russian Tsars had tried to deal with this problem, but all had failed to overcome the complexities involved. By 1830, Speransky and his section had compiled a mammoth 45 volumes. The first 40 volumes contained over 30,000 laws. The last five contained a detailed index and annexes. Speransky then set about producing a code, which contained only active laws, collected and listed by subject. Speransky had wanted to produce a detailed commentary to accompany the code, but Nicholas vetoed this on the grounds that the laws should speak for themselves. However, Speransky did borrow concepts from foreign legal systems to make the code more coherent. Thus in some ways he circumvented the Tsar's prohibition on a commentary. This code was made up of 15 volumes and was completed at the beginning of 1833. It was put into effect in 1835. From that point onwards the code was regularly revised and updated. The Russian legal system at last had a firm, clear basis from which to work. Its application in practice fell short of Speransky's hopes, but it did provide the foundation necessary for the establishment of a uniform legal system throughout Russia.

   * The Third Section controlled the political, or secret police. It was headed by General Benckendorf, who had been commander of the Guards under Alexander. On the grounds that the police were inefficient and attracted a very poor calibre of recruit, he suggested the formation of a ministry of police and the overhaul of the whole system. Nicholas, who had a deep distrust of ministries, but who sympathised

with the aims expressed, refused to set up a new ministry. Instead, he created the Corps of Gendarmes, to be administered by the Third Section under Benckendorf's command. The commander of the Third Section was determined that the new police should be of the highest possible calibre, and be respected and admired by the populace. Great efforts were made to give this new body a positive image and to separate them in everyone's mind from the ordinary police. The Gendarmes were given bright sky-blue uniforms with white gloves to emphasise their purity of purpose. Within three years Benckendorf reported to the Tsar that 'The Gendarmerie has become moral physician to the people. To it each comes with his ailments and despair.' Though reality fell somewhat short of this grand claim, the 'blue archangels' did win much support in their early years. They received complaints, they rooted out corrupt officials, they prepared cases against unjust landlords, and they even privately advocated progressive changes in the position of serfs. In their early years, therefore, the Gendarmes won much of the respect that Benckendorf sought for them and many of their top officials were welcomed in liberal circles. However, as time went on they concentrated more on their role as censors and as the suppressors of subversive ideas than on their roles as champions of justice and the enemies of corruption. They also exercised an increasingly repressive influence on education, especially after Uvarov's resignation (see page 46). This led to them being increasingly associated with the reactionary elements of Russian society.

   * The Fifth Section was created in 1836 to improve the administration of the state peasants. The aim was to make them more efficient producers, both for the benefit of the state as a whole and as an example for the landowners to follow with their serfs. Kiselev, another German who had been in Russian service since before 1812, was placed at the head of the new section. The following year, Nicholas overcame his dislike of ministries and created the Ministry of State Domains, with Kiselev at its head. He did so specifically to give weight to the project and to show the importance he attached to it.

   Kiselev headed the Ministry for the next 18 years and did make considerable progress. New land was surveyed and opened up to landless peasants. Loans were made readily available to the peasants to make improvements on their lands. New crops, particularly the potato, and improved breeding techniques were encouraged and supported. Hospitals, schools and churches were built to cater for over 200,000 peasants who were resettled on new land during this period. Kiselev has been much criticised because the main object of the exercise, to turn the state peasants into an efficient and productive group, did not succeed, and because of the authoritarian nature of his reforms. Resettlement was not voluntary, and many peasants naturally resented being forcibly moved. They also resented the changes in what they could and could not grow, which were largely forced upon them, and the much stricter control in general which Kiselev's officials imposed, often with little thought for winning the positive support of the peasants. There were periodic riots, particularly between 1841 and 1843, when the introduction of the potato was being forced on the peasants.

These drawbacks must be balanced against a consideration of the likely condition of the peasantry had these attempts at improvement not been made. Conditions would certainly not have been better. Kiselev did at least represent an attempt to bring about a planned improvement in their conditions. His officials also gathered valuable knowledge and experience of peasants' problems, which was to be of great value in helping to plan and implement the later reforms of Alexander II. Had the positive effects of these reforms been able to keep pace with the negative effects of rapid population growth, both Nicholas and Kiselev might have been forgiven for the heavy-handed nature of their implementation. As it was, population growth largely outstripped the positive benefits of reform, which therefore led to criticism and unrest rather than appreciation and stability.

* In terms of the economy in general, Nicholas also sought to make progress. Economic policy during this period was largely formulated by Kankrin, another German who had been in Russian service since 1797, and who had distinguished himself in 1812 as quartermaster-general. He was Minister of Finance from 1823 to 1844. Kankrin was a conservative who believed strongly in protecting domestic industries from foreign competition and in balancing the budget. He was determined to reduce the national debt and to stabilise the value of the rouble.

Kankrin was both reactionary and progressive. He opposed the development of a railway system, because he thought it would be of little advantage economically and would merely serve to encourage travel and the spread of unhealthy ideas. Indeed it is quite possible that no railway development would have taken place in this period, but for Nicholas's personal intervention. However, in other areas Kankrin was progressive. He set up various bodies to consult with Russian manufacturing and business interests, both to explain his plans and to take note of their comments. He fostered an expansion of technical and commercial education. His ministry encouraged and funded study abroad and he also reorganised the study of both mining and forestry.

Part of Kankrin's poor reputation stems from the fact that it was during this period that Russia fell so far behind western Europe (and particularly England) in terms of production. However, this was in many ways a product of the social system which existed in Russia. In every case considerable progress was made. Foreign trade increased by approximately 250 per cent during Nicholas's reign. What was static was Russia's share of world trade, which remained stable at about 3.7 per cent of the total. Russia increased production and trade at the same rate as the average increase for the rest of the world. What she did not do was to keep pace with the industrial revolution which took place in western Europe. But this she almost certainly could not have done without a major transformation in the nature and structure of Russian society.

Kankrin is also given little credit for his efforts to stabilise the currency and to reduce inflation. In fact he did make significant progress. By 1843 he had reduced the number of roubles in circulation to one quarter of their peak level. He had backed the currency firmly by establishing gold and silver reserves, thus stabilising its value at home and abroad, and he had significantly reduced the national debt. He had therefore established some degree of confidence and stability in the monetary system, which should have aided further growth and expansion. Kankrin retired in 1844 and died the next year. His successors could not match his efforts. Their inefficiency, coupled with the disastrous effects of the Crimean War, left the currency in an even worse situation than it had been in before Kankrin's reforms. Whilst it is almost certainly true, as his critics assert, that his tight fiscal control did little to free money for investment in industry, he did at least arrest the growing instability of the rouble. Whilst economists will continue to debate the nature of economic growth, a stable currency is generally held to be an important prerequisite for such growth. This Kankrin did achieve during his own period in office, even if his successors could not maintain that stability.

4   The Reactionary?

From the above it is perhaps not easy to see how Nicholas and his reign gained their reactionary reputation. This apparent anomaly can be explained by reference to four main factors. Nicholas expanded rigid centralised control of government. He insisted on conducting much of the activity of his administration in secret. His reign coincided with the rise of the intelligentsia who were by nature critical of his rule. Finally, he adopted as his main doctrine the idea of 'Orthodoxy, Autocracy, Nationality'.

The Polish revolt of 1830–1 has often been seen as a major turning point in Nicholas's reign. 1830 saw a wave of revolutionary activity in Europe. The July Revolution in Paris, which brought Louis-Philippe to the throne, was followed by the Belgian uprising in September against the Dutch, and unrest in Italy and Germany. This activity naturally worried Nicholas, who feared that its spread would threaten his own throne. He tried to coordinate international action against the revolutionaries but received very little support from other governments. He contemplated direct military action to stabilise affairs, but in late November 1830 he found that the spread of revolutionary ideas to his own empire had occurred, exactly as he had feared. The Poles rose in revolt against their Russian overlords. Constantine failed to control the situation and the Polish standing army supported the revolt. It took nine months to suppress the uprising and it cost many lives, including Constantine's, who died of cholera.

Nicholas was determined to control the Poles. He revoked the constitution and replaced it with a much more restrictive statute. Poland lost its right to a national assembly and a separate army. The Universities of Warsaw and Vilna were closed. In theory Poland retained a separate administration, but, from 1833 until after Nicholas's death, she was ruled under martial law and her administration was placed under increasingly tight Russian control. A deliberate and determined policy of 'russification' (the imposition of Russian ways, institutions and beliefs, and the eradication of local customs, institutions and beliefs) had begun.

* There is little doubt that the events of 1830–1 surprised and worried Nicholas. The appointment of Uvarov as Minister of Education in 1833 and the adoption of the doctrine of 'Official Nationality' have been seen as evidence that Nicholas decided on a policy of increased internal repression. Yet Uvarov, though certainly a conservative, was if anything more liberal than his immediate predecessors, and did at least have a genuine interest and respect for education. Equally there was nothing in the doctrine of 'Official Nationality' to suggest a move away from that which Nicholas had been expounding since the beginning of his reign. It was adopted because it fitted so closely to his own ideas. Uvarov succinctly summed up 'Official Nationality' as 'Orthodoxy, Autocracy, Nationality'. These three elements were meant to provide the basis and justification for maintaining Russia against harmful influences for change, especially of a revolutionary or democratic nature.

'Orthodoxy' was taken to have two main elements. The first emphasised the relationship between Tsar, God and the Orthodox Church, with the Tsar as the rightful, undisputed ruler placed on his throne 'by God's special grace'. The second element centred on the precepts of the Church as a guide to human action. Piety was taken as the main yardstick in human behaviour and life in 'this world' was not held to be nearly as important as life in the 'next world'.

'Autocracy' represented the traditional Russian view of the total submission to the Tsar of all his subjects. The 'Little Father' was completely responsible for his people's spiritual and physical welfare. From above, he and only he could really see what was best for them. He might need to be harsh on occasion, but what he did, he did for the benefit of all. He had to protect them from themselves in case they allowed themselves to be infected by foreign ideas such as freedom and democracy. He had to keep Russia strong and powerful lest the Empire succumb to foreign threats to the detriment of all his 'children'.

'Nationality' meant essentially the promotion of Russian culture and institutions as something to be treasured and preserved, the fostering of a patriotic spirit and the distinct identity of Russia separate from the rest of Europe. This spirit was taken by the more extreme supporters of nationality as the justification for demanding the russification of all the lands and people on the edges of the Empire. Whilst Nicholas may have been pleased at the patriotic nature of these demands, the fact that he resisted them is important. Above all Nicholas desired a calm and well-ordered society. He would not introduce change unless it was necessary and certain to bring clear benefits. Thus Finland and the Baltic states were left virtually untouched, because they were considered loyal. However, where there was revolt or open opposition, as in Poland and Transcaucasia, local institutions were largely swept away to be replaced by Russian institutions and governors.

* This desire to ensure that change was only introduced when it was clearly necessary runs deep throughout Nicholas's reign. It was coupled with a strong desire to prevent the general populace from coming into contact with new ideas for fear of what their spread might lead to. This desire resulted in a proliferation of secret committees, which were established throughout his reign. The first such committee was established in December 1826. Its task was to consider the state papers left by Alexander, and the condition of Russia in general, and to make suggestions as to what should be altered to improve the situation which the Decembrist report had highlighted (see page 35). The committee was so secret that Kankrin, who was called before it to give advice on financial considerations, was not even informed of the nature and purpose of the committee. The committee laboured for six painstaking years. It only produced very minor suggestions for modifying the existing system, yet even these recommendations were not put into practice. Nicholas subsequently set up further secret committees with more clearly defined tasks. The very secrecy of these committees made it appear that Nicholas was more reactionary than he actually was. It appeared to the majority that he was doing nothing and considering no change. In fact he was almost constantly considering change, though always from the top and under his personal control.

* Nine committees in all were set up to examine the question of serfdom. These committees were also kept secret in case rumours of emancipation led to unrest. Nicholas did enact several measures to improve the situation of the serfs. In 1827 he set out clear limitations to landowners' rights to send serfs to Siberia. In 1833 he prohibited the selling of serfs by public auction, the splitting up of serf families and the use of serfs without land to obtain credit. In 1842 it was made technically easier for serfs to buy their freedom. Finally, in 1847, serfs were given the right to buy their freedom if their village was sold at public auction. This might appear to be an impressive list, but in practice it made little or no difference to the great majority of serfs. They were largely unable to take advantage of their new 'rights'. Nicholas knew that real change had to come. He believed that serfdom

failed on both economic and moral grounds, but he was prevented from taking firm action in part by the concerted opposition he faced. However, two other factors were arguably of greater significance in limiting the measures he took. The need to prevent the unrest that new ideas might generate, and the perceived need to bolster the landowning nobility (who were decreasing steadily in number and power as they sank as a class into increasing debt) were always in the forefront of his mind. His feelings are clearly summarised in the following passage from his speech to the State Council in 1842:

1 There is no question that serfdom in its present state in our country is an evil, palpable and obvious to everyone. However, to attack it now would be, of course, an even more disastrous evil . . . The Pugachev rebellion showed how far mob violence can go.
5 [Pugachev led a two-year peasant revolt in the 1770s.] Fortunately, later occurrences of this sort have always, until now, been suppressed . . . But we must not conceal from ourselves the fact that current ideas are not the same as those that existed previously, and it is clear to every reasonable observer that the present
10 situation cannot last forever.

This fear of instituting real change severely limited the possibilities open to Nicholas. Whilst maintaining an overall system as inherently rigid as an autocracy, there is limited scope for ameliorating the intrinsic effects of that system.

* The most stringent criticism of Nicholas's reign is usually reserved for the fields of education and censorship. Uvarov was Minister of Education from 1833 to 1849. Along with the Third Section, he was also in charge of censorship. Uvarov was an intellectual with a great love of the classics, who had resigned his post as head of the St Petersburg educational region in 1819 in protest at repressive actions taken against the University. Though Uvarov might have been liberal in comparison with his predecessors, he was conservative even by Russian standards. He was a staunch defender of serfdom and believed firmly that education should be tailored to the status of the people receiving it. He sought firm control over education throughout Russia. Private schools and private tutors were made directly responsible to the state for what they taught. A large inspectorate was built up to ensure that teaching conformed to the rules laid down by his ministry. Above all he wished to prevent the spread of 'improper ideas'. He wanted to instil in the young a respect for Russian institutions and a love of their country. At first many people felt that Uvarov was making positive moves, and he did actively encourage developments in the 'safe' areas of scientific and technical research. However, as he steadily increased the centralised nature of his control over the education system, and as the list of restrictions grew, the number and volume of his critics steadily increased.

It was censorship which aroused the most opposition. Responsibility for censorship was shared between the Ministry of Education and the Third Section. It was often as arbitrary as it had been in the latter days of Alexander's reign. A cookery book was not allowed to mention 'free air' because it sounded too revolutionary, and any discussion of social issues was frowned upon. Although censorship raised a great deal of opposition, it did not become as all encompassing as it had been in the final years of Alexander until the end of Nicholas's reign. This is perhaps best illustrated by the following extract from an anonymous article which was passed by the censor in 1836. It was published in the Moscow periodical, *The Telescope*, as a *Philosophical Letter* from 'Necropolis' (The City of the Dead).

1 We have never progressed in keeping with other peoples of the world [but] exist as if in banishment outside the times, untouched by the universal education of mankind . . .

   [In Europe] each person is fully possessed of his rights and
5 easily gathers the ideas that have spread throughout society and uses them for his advantage . . . They are the concepts of duty, justice, law, and order . . .

   Despite the fact that we are called Christians, we did not move when Chistianity, leaving the past behind it, progressed along the
10 path solemnly indicated by the Divine Founder. While the world entirely rebuilt itself, we built nothing but continued in our mud huts . . .

   Though our limited mental habits, traditions, and memories do not link us to any peoples of the world . . . we still belong to the
15 Western world. This link still makes our destiny dependent on European society. Therefore the more we try to affiliate ourselves with it, the better off we shall be . . .

One contemporary saw the letter as a 'merciless cry of reproach and bitterness against Russia'. It was a cry which was to be echoed by a growing group of 'Westernisers' and liberals.

Nicholas reacted in a characteristically thorough and resolute manner. The censor who had passed the article was dismissed. *The Telescope* was closed down and its publisher was sent into exile. The author of the letter, Chadaev, was discovered, declared insane and confined to house arrest, though he was well treated in his captivity. In a few months, after renouncing the more extreme of his views, he was allowed back into circulation and was once more prominent at intellectual gatherings. Because periodicals (journals) were perhaps generally more careful about how far they went, only three were actually closed down during the whole of Nicholas's reign. Censorship did not actually disrupt the intellectual pursuits of the intelligentsia very much. If anything, it acted as a spur to them. What censorship did do was to prevent the free spread of ideas outside the narrow confines of this group. It was also very severe in individual cases, especially in the case of the daily press, which suffered more than the periodicals. It was therefore effective in promoting the view of the Tsar and his administration as narrow and repressive in outlook, rather than actually stifling debate as was intended.

 * The *Philosophical Letter* pointed to the growth of two increasingly important and influential groups in Russian society: the 'Westernisers' and the 'Slavophiles'. The Westernisers, mostly liberal in makeup, held that Russia had much to learn from western Europe about social organisation and government. They pointed to Peter the Great as a Tsar who had moved Russia in a modern and progressive direction to the benefit of all. The Slavophiles were closer to Nicholas's ideas on Orthodoxy and Autocracy. They believed in the inherent superiority of Orthodoxy as a moral force. They saw the Tsar, an autocratic Tsar, as the unifying symbol of the Russian state. They embodied a type of romantic spiritualism, which saw in the peasant commune an idealised form of society based on fraternal love, freedom and spiritual purity. They believed that the commune had developed from Slavic traditions under the guiding hand of the Orthodox Church. They also felt that further development of the commune would enable Russia to avoid unhealthy western influences, which to them rested on an unholy, and far too worldly basis of individualism, rationalism and competition. Slavophiles wanted progress, but firmly within Russian traditions as they saw them. To them, Peter the Great was a dangerous aberration.

The Westernisers' view is perhaps best summarised by Belinsky in his *Letter to Gogol*, in which he criticised the author, whose previous works he had respected and supported, for praising existing Russian society.

1 ... you failed to realise that Russia sees her salvation, not in mysticism, nor in asceticism, nor pietism, but in the successes of civilisation, enlightenment, and humanity ... I leave it to your conscience to admire the divine beauty of autocracy (it is both safe
5 and profitable), but continue to admire it judiciously from your beautiful faraway; at close quarters it is not so attractive and not so safe.

The letter was not officially published for over 50 years, but it became widely discussed inside Russia and came to the attention of the Third Section. The grapevine of the intelligentsia was efficient and effective at carrying the news that it wished to carry. Ideas were also spread under a number of guises in various journals. Belinsky, for example, had successfully put forward his ideas over the previous eight years as the chief literary critic of a St Petersburg journal.

Censorship was annoying. It was arbitrary and unfair. It was a focal point for opposition. It certainly did not encourage free and open debate, but it was not until after 1848, as in other areas of Russian life discussed above, that it really began to bite.

5 The Last Seven Years

It was the latter part of Nicholas's reign which was in reality a stern period of repression. The rebellions which swept across Europe during 1848 worried leaders of all political complexions. Nicholas, being the most autocratic, had perhaps most reason to be concerned. This concern was increased by the fact that Russia's two main conservative allies, Prussia and Austria, were now ruled by ageing and increasingly indecisive leaders. This had prompted Nicholas to say: 'Once we were three, but now we are one and a half. I don't count Prussia and Austria counts for only a half.' The first results of the revolutions confirmed his worst fears. Frederick William of Prussia compromised with the rebels, and Metternich was relieved of office in Austria and was replaced by liberal influence. As the tide of revolt seemed to spread throughout Europe, Nicholas even asked Queen Victoria to stand with him against these dangerous and unholy movements. Predictably, Victoria declined the invitation.

Internal events served to increase Nicholas's fears. There was a severe cholera epidemic and the worst crop failure in 30 years, which led to the price of bread more than doubling. Nicholas once more took firm and decisive action. 400,000 troops were moved to the western borders to prevent the spread of anarchy. Another secret committee was set up to root out any subversive influence. Censorship was rigidly enforced. Gogol's works were not allowed to be re-published. Phrases such as 'sovereign remedy' and 'forces of nature' were removed from textbooks. Almost all foreign fiction was proscribed, including Andersen's fairy tales. Newspapers were strictly limited in what they could report, especially in terms of foreign news.

The Third Section uncovered the activities of 'The Petrashevsky Circle'. This group was accused of revolutionary conspiracy. In April 1849, 39 members of the circle were arrested. But after extensive interrogation and investigation no real evidence of a revolutionary conspiracy could be produced. The 'Circle' had merely met regularly to discuss contemporary problems. In the prevailing atmosphere that was enough. Twenty-one of those arrested were sentenced to death. Nicholas determined to make the most out of the case, and staged a dramatic last-second reprieve for the condemned men. An *aide* galloped in to Semenovsky Square to announce that the Tsar had decided to exercise clemency and spare their lives, just as the executions were about to take place. This theatrical reprieve was meant to warn of the dangers of revolutionary activity, but at the same time to show how merciful the Tsar was. It had the opposite result. The intelligentsia saw the affair as merely an example of unnecessary cruelty, putting the 21 young men through needless anguish and mental torment merely for effect.

At one stage it looked as if the universities might even be closed down. Uvarov rose to their defence, but the secret committee distrusted his motives and he was persuaded to resign. He was replaced by the utterly subservient Shikmatov, who boasted that 'I have no thought, no will of my own – I am a blind instrument of the will of my sovereign'. The universities were not closed down, but they were strictly controlled in terms of both curriculum and admissions. Student numbers fell by 25 per cent to 3600 over the next five years. Shikmatov stated that education should be based 'not on reason, but on religious truths connected with theology'.

Censorship increased: by 1850 there were twelve separate bodies with censorship duties. Turgenev was placed under house arrest merely for writing an obituary of Gogol. Even the Slavophiles were refused permission to publish a set of articles putting forward their views, on the grounds that, though they might be suitable for discussion by experts, they might be misinterpreted by a wider audience. This further alienated the intelligentsia, although on the surface all appeared calm.

Abroad, Nicholas succeeded in helping to limit the impact of the 1848 revolutions. He granted a loan of six million roubles to help prop up the Austrian regime. He firmly put down a nationalist revolt in Moldavia-Wallachia. In 1849 he sent 150,000 troops into Hungary to help crush the rebellion led by Kossuth. This not only enabled the new Austrian ruler to regain control of Hungary, but also allowed the Austrians to free troops in order to pacify their Italian possessions. In 1850 Nicholas managed to persuade the Prussians to end their plans for a German 'Union' and accept the status quo. Though Russian actions were probably not of overriding importance in stemming the revolutionary movements across Europe, they certainly helped to do so. To many it appeared that Russia alone was stable on the tide of unrest in Europe, and was at the peak of her powers.

* This illusion was soon to be shattered by the Crimean War of 1854–6. The real weakness of the Russian Empire was starkly exposed. The army was beautifully prepared for the parade ground, but it was neither equipped nor prepared to fight a modern war. Russia did not have the necessary industrial and economic base to supply the army properly, and did not have an effective transport system or an efficient bureaucracy to organise and move what supplies there were. The result was ignominious defeat. Nicholas did not survive to see the end of the war. He caught a winter chill but refused to rest and maintained his normal strenuous programme of inspections and work. The strain

proved too great and he developed pneumonia and rapidly declined. He died on 18 February 1855. As one commentator recorded: 'A long and, one must admit, a joyless page in the history of the Russian Empire has been written out to the last word.'

6 Assessment

With the exception of Marxist analysts, historians generally agree on the importance of Nicholas as a strong and determined centralising presence. However, they disagree over what were the most important aspects of his reign: the relative stagnation of the economy, the growth of the bureaucracy, the repression of new ideas, or the deliberate concentration on the policy of 'Orthodoxy, Autocracy, Nationality'. Most opt for the latter on the grounds that this policy embodied all that was negative in Nicholas's reign. Rigid repression did not really grip the country until after 1848, but by then, although Russia appeared strong and vigorous, the real damage had been done. Nicholas gave no positive new direction to the country when it desperately needed it. He sought to improve what existed, but was governed by his fear of new ideas and his belief in the intrinsic values of the old ways and the old system. His reluctance to delegate responsibility led to him taking on so much work himself that he was unable to make an effective impact on the implementation of his policies. He always tried to see for himself that his wishes were carried out, but in a country of the vast size of Russia this led at best to a superficiality which allowed graft, corruption and inefficiency to grow despite his best efforts. More importantly, his unshakable belief in autocracy and traditional ways prevented Russia from developing.

His legacy to his successor was a heavy one. It contained all the problems which had existed on his accession: an increasingly backward economy; an inefficient bureaucracy; an outmoded serf system; a limited education system; and a nobility which was moving rapidly towards bankruptcy. However, by the end of his reign these problems had worsened considerably because of the lack of effective action in the face of rapid population growth inside Russia, and the rapid industrial expansion elsewhere. This legacy also contained the developing basis for a police state in the shape of the Third Section, and the basis of a radical opposition in the intelligentsia, who were largely alienated from the Romanov dynasty and increasingly disenchanted with autocracy. Effective change had been held back for 30 years. As the Crimean War showed only too clearly, change was long overdue.

1825	The Decembrist revolt	1825

1825	Harsh treatment of the Decembrists Removal of the more reactionary members of the government	1826

1826	Limited reform	1830

1830	The Polish revolt	1830

1830	Arbitrary censorship Tighter control over education Growth of the third section Orthodoxy, autocracy and nationality The secret committees	Legal reform Economic reform Reform of the state peasants Limited serf reform Administration improves in some ways	1848

1848	Rigid repression	1854

1854	The Crimean War	1855

Summary – Nicholas I 1825–55

Making notes on Nicholas I

Your notes on this chapter should give you an understanding of what Nicholas I sought to achieve. He wanted progress, but not liberal progress. He wanted a progress which left the essential traditions and nature of Russia untainted by 'pernicious' foreign influences. He wanted to improve the efficiency and strength of the country and to improve the life of its inhabitants, but not at the expense of the autocracy, which he felt was of central importance in maintaining the Russian state. The conflict between these two aims is a key factor in understanding this period.

The following headings should help you to identify the main points:

1.   The Decembrist Revolt
1.1. Confusion over the succession
1.2. Inaction over planned revolt
1.3. The day of the revolt
2.   The Military Tsar
2.1. The nature of the Tsar
2.2. Action over the Decembrists
2.3. Plans for action
3.   The Chancery, Planning and Progress
3.1. Legal reform
3.2. The Third Section
3.3. The state peasants
3.4. The economy
4.   The Reactionary?
4.1. The Polish revolt
4.2. 'Orthodoxy, Autocracy and Nationality'
4.3. The secret committees
4.4. The serf question
4.5. Education and censorship
4.6. Westernisers and Slavophiles
5.   The Last Seven Years
5.1. The impact of the 1848 rebellions
6.   Assessment

Answering essay questions on Nicholas I

The evidence in this chapter should enable you to answer any questions on Nicholas I which do not deal directly with foreign policy. Examples of the most common types of questions on Nicholas I are:

1. '"A merely repressive ruler." Assess the validity of this judgement on Nicholas I's reign.'
2. 'Explain the changes which took place in the internal policies and conditions in Russia between 1825 and 1850.'

The first question concentrates on the nature of Nicholas's rule. It asks you to look at his reign and decide whether repression was the only major characteristic of it. Your notes should show you that his reign embodied far more than mere repression. To answer the question you would need to consider the repressive aspects of his reign and show how he might therefore be described as repressive. But you should then go on to consider the other aspects of his reign. These might include his concern over the state peasants and the serfs, his drive for efficiency, his generous treatment of the Finns in contrast to the Poles and the moves towards a balanced budget.

The second question, though using much the same information, asks you to concentrate on the reason for the changes in attitude which took place during Nicholas's reign. This requires you to identify when, if at all, such changes took place, to illustrate the nature of these changes and then to explain their cause. To add depth to your answer you should also consider the idea (even if you reject it) that the whole of his reign can be seen in terms of the often conflicting aims of a desire for progress whilst maintaining the autocracy and traditional Russian values.

You should now be able to tackle a comparative type of question asking you to contrast Alexander I and Nicholas I. An example of this type of question is:

3. 'Was Nicholas I significantly more repressive than Alexander I?'

You need to be particularly careful when dealing with the idea of significance. What criteria will you use, and are there any other criteria which might be equally legitimate in order to decide on significance? It would be beneficial to draw up a detailed essay plan for this question and to discuss your results with others to try to see why your plan may differ from theirs.

Source-based questions on Nicholas I

1   The Decembrist Revolt
Carefully read the extract from Nicholas's personal account of the day of the revolt on pages 32–3. Answer the following questions:
a)   How does Nicholas justify allowing the 'Guards Grenadiers' to join the rebels? (1 mark)

b) What does the fourth paragraph reveal about Nicholas's priorities? (3 marks)
c) What does Nicholas give as his reason for finally deciding to fire on the rebels? (2 marks)
d) Is there any evidence within this extract to suggest that it is not a completely open and candid account? Explain your answer. (4 marks)

2   The Nature and Priorities of Nicholas I
Study the extract from Queen Victoria on page 34 and the extract from Nicholas's manifesto on page 36. Answer the following questions:
a) Make a list of the positive and negative qualities attributed to Nicholas by Queen Victoria. (4 marks)
b) Do the list and the extract appear to provide a balanced view? Explain your answer. (5 marks)
c) Does Victoria's judgement help to explain any of the problems which Nicholas faced during his reign? Explain your answer. (6 marks)
d) Does the passage from Nicholas's manifesto back up any of the statements made by Victoria? Explain you answer. (5 marks)

3   The Serf Question
Carefully read the extract from Nicholas's speech to the State Council in 1842 given on page 42. Answer the following questions:
a) What is Nicholas's view of serfdom? (4 marks)
b) What reason does he give for inaction? (3 marks)
c) What might he have hoped to achieve by giving this speech? (3 marks)

4   The Westernisers
Carefully study the extract from the *Philosophical Letter* given on page 43 and the extract from Belinsky's *Letter to Gogol* given on page 44. Answer the following questions:
a) What criticisms of Russian society are made in the *Philosophical Letter*? (3 marks)
b) What solutions does it propose? (3 marks)
c) What criticisms does Belinsky make of Russian society? (3 marks)
d) What solutions does he propose? (3 marks)
e) Discuss the similarities/differences between your two sets of answers. What form do they take? Explain the similarities and differences. (8 marks)

CHAPTER 4

The Emancipation of the Serfs

1 Alexander II

Alexander II had one great advantage over his father when he came to the throne; he had been prepared for the task. Nicholas had been determined that his son should be fully trained for the task of ruling Russia. He had planned his son's education in all its aspects with great care. In this area he had been rather more successful than in many others.

Alexander was 37 at the time of his father's death. He had received a broad education, had travelled widely and had been given extensive practical experience in government. This was to stand him in good stead. He had been the first member of the imperial family to visit Siberia. This visit had given him some understanding of the conditions suffered by those in exile. He had served on the Council of State for 14 years and on numerous lesser committees, including the secret committees concerned with serfdom and the railways. This gave him a depth of knowledge about Russia's problems. Alexander had also been left in charge of state affairs on a number of occasions in his father's absence, which had provided him with direct experience of the problems of ruling the country.

Alexander was rather more humane and sensitive than his father and inspired rather less awe in those around him. Nonetheless he believed firmly in autocracy as the way forward for his people. He was patriotic, religious and conservative in outlook, but his experience of government had convinced him of the need for change in many aspects of the structure of the state. To come to the throne in the midst of the Crimean War, which was in effect a disastrous defeat, may seem an inauspicious beginning to his reign. Paradoxically, however, it was to aid him in his desire to bring about real change in Russia.

2 The Crimean Effect

'War is the Locomotive of History.' Trotsky's dictum, like many others, may be rather over-used. However, if the history of any country lends support to this view, it is surely the history of Russia. After military defeat at the end of the seventeenth century, Peter the Great had almost completely remodelled the Russian state. Catherine the Great had brought in almost equally radical changes under pressure from external events. Again in 1905, after defeat by Japan, a major change in the structure of the Russian state was to be attempted, and it has been powerfully argued that World War I was the prime cause of the demise of the Romanov dynasty.

The Crimean War also acted as a force for change. The structure of the Russian state was examined and found to be wanting. It was not capable of competing with the more modern European powers. Why was this? A significant clue is given in a message of encouragement from Alexander to his generals, in 1855:

> 1 Do not lose heart; remember 1812 and put your trust in God. Sebastopol is not Moscow and the Crimea is not Russia. Two years after the Moscow fire, our victorious troops were in Paris. We are the same Russians and God is with us.

The last sentence is particularly important. Russia in 1855 was indeed virtually the same as Russia in 1812. In 1812, Russia was backward and, to gain victory, needed the aid of the Russian winter to destroy half a million of Napoleon's troops. Progress had been made since then, but it was very limited in comparison to the European nations she faced. Comparatively Russia was now even more 'backward', and the 'Russian winter' was not as severe in the Crimea as it was around Moscow. The result was ignominious defeat. It was this defeat which prompted action. Nicholas had died at a time when the Russian position in the Crimea seemed hopeless. In reality it probably was, but, understandably, the new Tsar did not want his first act to be one of surrender. Indeed, he felt deeply that to do so would be to dishonour the name of Russia. Instead he decided to pursue the war with renewed vigour. At first Russian fortunes did seem to improve, but, at the beginning of September 1855, after 349 days of siege, Sebastopol fell. Alexander still refused to negotiate an end to the war and Russia struggled on for a further four months. In the end, however, the threat of Austria joining the war finally forced Alexander to agree to a peace, although not until the day before the Austrian ultimatum expired. This disaster clearly pointed to the fact that Russia was a backward state, unable to stand up to the more modern European powers. For perhaps the first time in Russia, the majority of those with influence felt that some real change was needed. Alexander's first priority was 'Emancipation'.

3 Why Emancipation of the Serfs?

Defeat in the Crimea understandably affected Alexander more deeply than most. He saw the protection and maintenance of the great Russian state as his primary God-given duty. It was up to him to restore Russia's prestige and power. He felt that the condition and structure of the Russian peasantry was a crucial factor in Russia's weakness. Both Alexander I and Nicholas I had recognised this before when they had attempted to address the issue of the serfs, but little significant change had actually been effected. The Crimean War highlighted the failings in

Russian society and once more focused attention upon the problem of serfdom. As the prominent Slavophile, Samarin, noted during the war:

1 At the head of our domestic problems which we must tackle stands – as a portent for the future and as an obstacle which precludes at the present time a substantial improvement of anything whatever – the question of serfdom.

The reason for this conclusion is clear. Even as late as the middle of the nineteenth century, one can argue that the Russian peasant was Russia. The peasant paid most of the taxes, produced the grain which was Russia's most valuable export, produced the food which Russians ate, and formed over 80 per cent of the population. Tolstoy perhaps best characterised the nature of Russia at this time, when he described it as a peasant country with a superficial veneer of urban sophistication. Almost half of the peasants were serfs. Their problems were therefore also the problems of the Russian state.

  * Serfdom was failing on almost all counts. It was failing the serfs themselves and it was failing the nobility. More importantly, perhaps, it was failing the state, both in term of economic progress and in terms of stability.

Serfdom was failing the serfs largely because the system was unable to deliver an increased rate of productivity which matched the rapid population growth. Russia's population doubled between 1800 and 1858 (see page 5). By the 1840s, 30 per cent of the peasants in the

'Gambling for souls' – engraving by Gustav Doré 1854

north-eastern provinces had to earn their living away from the village. As the population grew, the serfs found their traditional poverty descending to an increasingly intolerable level. Serfdom was failing the nobility in that the system simply no longer provided them with an adequate income to meet their needs in a changing economic climate. The nobility were therefore falling into increasing debt. By 1860, 60 per cent of all private serfs were mortgaged to the state and over 50 per cent of land values were similarly mortgaged. The system was also failing the state because it did not encourage innovation and experiment in both industry and agriculture. This was held to be at least in part responsible for the relative stagnation of the Russian economy in comparison with America and the nations of western Europe. Serfdom no longer even provided stability. With the rapid population growth, the limited amount of land for the peasants to work and the slow increase in productivity, there was often not enough food. This led to a growing tide of unrest. Outbreaks of peasant disobedience, which could be anything from 'insubordination' to full-scale revolt, were rising steadily. Between 1826 and 34 there were 148 outbreaks; between 1835 and 44, 216 and between 1845 and 54, 348.

For a combination of these reasons Alexander felt that the serf question was of central importance to the future wellbeing of the Russian state. The serfs were a key factor in domestic production. They were also the major source of recruits to the army: the same army which had just been so ignominiously defeated. Alexander was intent on improving Russia's economic and industrial performance. He saw the inertia resulting from the serf system as a major obstacle. The moral aspect of the issue was also of increasing importance as new ideas and standards spread from the west. Coupled to this was the growing threat to the social order of the country as the system increasingly failed to satisfy the economic needs of landlord and serf alike. Alexander felt that the system itself needed to be changed if these problems were to be remedied. He believed that this change was necessary if he was to make Russia a strong and respected force in the world again – a task which he saw as his God-given duty.

4 The Condition of the Peasantry

The peasants were divided into two categories: state peasants and landlords' peasants (serfs). These two categories of peasant were distributed in almost direct relation to geographical area. Around Moscow and in the western provinces the proportion of serfs was over 50 per cent of the population. The further one moved north, south or east, away from the direct influence of the old Muscovite state, the less serfdom one encountered.

Both groups were technically bound to the land, which meant that they could not leave without permission. In reality, however, the serf was bound to the land, whereas the state peasant enjoyed varying degrees of freedom. The state peasants were mainly the inhabitants of the Crown Estates (confiscated from the Church in the eighteenth century), or were non-Russians such as Tartars and nomads. They could not leave their village without permission, but they were largely free to indulge in whatever gainful activity they wished as long as they paid their taxes. Although they had not owned their land until after 1837, they had long since acted as if they did. They did have a large measure of control over their lives, albeit within the peculiar and restrictive confines of the Russian legal system, and subject to the vagaries of the local governors, who were often more responsive to a bribe than to reason and argument.

* Serfs were in a very different position. Their lives were dominated by the *mir*, the family, and the noble who had control over them. The *mir* was a collective unit, which made almost all local decisions over land use and distribution, including when crops should be sown and gathered. Land was normally worked on the 'three field system' (one fallow, with different crops in the other two in rotation) and was normally distributed in strips. Some areas in the village were naturally more fertile than others. To try to ensure a fair distribution of land a family's holding would be made up of strips of land in good and bad areas. Land was also often periodically redistributed as a family's circumstances changed. This may have been fair, but it entailed a number of serious disadvantages. The strip system led to inefficient use of land, and periodic redistribution tended to mitigate against improving the land and adopting innovative techniques. The *mir* council was made up of the heads of families and it normally elected one leader or 'Elder'. There was little or no opportunity to appeal against the decision of the council or Elder. Yet for all these defects, most Serfs saw the *mir* as a blessing rather than a burden. It gave them a collective identity, which is captured clearly in the saying: 'a Russian taken individually will not get into heaven, but there is no way of keeping out an entire village'.

The head of the family (normally an extended family of three generations) had almost complete control over the members of the group. He represented their views at the *mir* council and had the final say in decisions affecting the family. Sons could not leave home, marry or engage in a trade without permission.

The noble could determine when and to whom his serfs would marry. This usually meant early marriage as more children were still seen as a way of increasing revenue rather than an increasing drain on limited resources. He could take serfs into domestic service at will, or indeed ask almost anything else of them, but stories of sexual license and sadistic cruelty, though true in part, were certainly the exception rather than the rule.

* Serfs were divided into two categories: those who paid rent (*obrok*)

and those who paid in labour (*corvée* or *barschina*). Those who paid *barschina* were in theory limited to a maximum of three days' work per week on their lord's land, but they had no one to complain to if this was exceeded. The short length of the summer in much of Russia meant that all the work on their own land and their master's land had to be done in a very limited period. This commonly led to feverish bouts of activity with an 18 or 20-hour day at work, followed by relative idleness during the long winter.

However, those who paid rent (*obrok*) could be just as badly off. They did often have some degree of freedom to work at whatever trade they wished, but their masters were not above encouraging cottage industry and then varying the rent according to the profits or their own need. Their need was not always matched by the serfs' productivity. In theory at least, the only action not open to the owner of a serf was murder. There is evidence to suggest that even this occasionally occurred. This wide-ranging power could lead to great misery, as was illustrated by E. N. Vodovosova in her childhood memories of serfdom in Russia.

1 Not far from our estate there was another smaller one belonging to three sisters called Tonchev ... Lala was the favourite; her sisters considered her a beauty, dressed her up, spoiled her, and never gave up hope of seeing her married. With Lala's dowry in
5 mind they tortured their serfs by keeping them at the embroidery frames and looms day and night. The peasants who belonged to the Tonchevs not only had a heavier 'Master's Duty' than was done on other estates, but if the weather was good and Mila's hay not cut they had to work even on 'peasants' days'. This apart the
10 women had very heavy duties both summer and winter: each had to provide for Lala's dowry a set amount of linen, had to weave with cotton, thread and wool, and had to embroider towels and sheets. In the summer loads of berries and mushrooms had to be gathered for the sisters – and in fact the peasants were so busy all
15 the year round that they had no time left for their own work. Hardly a day passed without someone being whipped by way of punishment: for the smallest fault, offending peasants were beaten by the bailiff in the presence of the two elder sisters ...
    Things came to a head in an incident which took place in early
20 autumn when the sisters were on their way home from a party. They were driving in a carriage with the coachman; it was about midnight and very dark, and they had some three miles of forest to cross. After about a mile they were suddenly surrounded by a crowd; some took the horses by the reins and pulled the
25 coachman down, whilst others pulled the sisters out of the carriage. Lala and the coachman were bound and gagged and dragged to the side of the road whilst Mila and Dia were severely

thrashed . . . A few months after this incident, the sisters' newly
finished house was burnt to the ground. They had already started
30 to pack, ready for the move. This time there was plenty of
evidence, but the man who had set fire to the house escaped the
same night and was never found.

This was fairly typical of the problems which could and did arise. But
these problems were not new.

* Why then did emancipation not come sooner? Fear of change and
vested interest are key factors. Any real change would have involved
loss of land and service for the nobility. Although it is easy to say now
that the system was failing them, it is not surprising that the uncertainty over what would, and should, replace serfdom led to inaction. Fear
of what change might bring dominated the thinking of the majority,
and led to an inertia which was difficult to overcome. There was also an
intense desire to avoid what the Russian élite saw as the weaknesses and
problems that freedom had brought in western countries. Coupled to
this was a very real fear that the autocracy itself might be swept away if
such changes were begun.

Another important factor was the attitude of the peasants themselves.
At best it can be described as fatalistic. Their horizon barely stretched
beyond the village. Indeed, travellers reported that both distance and
the existence of other countries outside Russia were barely conceivable
to many of them. They did not associate their problems with the Tsar,
or with the 'System', but rather with corrupt local officials and
landlords. Their anger, when it was occasionally aroused, tended,
therefore, to be directed at something they could comprehend – their
immediate local environment. Finally, although their condition was in
many ways severe, for the vast majority it was not sufficiently severe to
promote outright despair. The following passage was written by a
British traveller in Russia who was far from sympathetic to the idea of
serfdom.

1 On the whole . . . so far at least as mere food and lodging are
concerned, the Russian peasant is not as badly off as the poor man
amongst ourselves . . . he never knows the misery to which the
Irish peasant is exposed . . . Not in Ireland only, but in parts of
5 Great Britain usually considered to be exempt from the miseries
of Ireland, we have witnessed wretchedness compared with which
the condition of the Russian boor is luxury . . . Let it not be
supposed, however, that, because we admit the Russian peasant
to be in many respects more comfortable than our own, we
10 therefore consider his lot as, on the whole, more enviable than
that of the peasant in a free country like ours. The distance
between them is wide – immeasurable; but it can be accounted for
in one single word – the British peasant has rights; the Russian
has none!

This was true. However, the concept of 'rights' is very abstract. The majority of Russian peasants neither understood nor, even if they had some vague understanding, were interested in the idea. They did not like to be mistreated, but the threat of starvation was of greater concern to the majority. They had suffered both for as long as they could remember. As various groups of revolutionaries were to find to their disappointment over the next 60 years, peasants did not have the time, the inclination nor possibly the conceptual grasp to worry about 'rights'. They were interested in the land and the food it provided. And, in the case of the serfs, in ridding themselves of the burden of the landlords whom they had to support. The serfs' condition limited both their horizons and their perspectives. They had little stake in society and therefore acted as a block to progress on many fronts.

5   The Road to Emancipation

How then was Alexander II able to introduce emancipation where his predecessors had failed so completely? Firstly he used Russia's bitter defeat to underline the need for change. He argued that if Russia was to make economic and social progress, serfdom must end. In this he was helped by the activities of the intellectuals over the preceding 30 years. They had not actually convinced many people, but they had created the intellectual climate in which change of this sort was seen as a positive and progressive move. This feeling had been reinforced by the fact that Nicholas had repeatedly stated that at some point serfdom must be abolished. Secondly, Alexander used the growing unrest amongst the serfs to play deliberately on fears of revolution from below. This was successful despite the fact that it seems very unlikely that most peasants actually wanted or would have even grasped such a complex concept as revolution. Finally, with these two factors weakening opposition to change, he was prepared to put the full weight of his autocratic power behind the drive towards emancipation.

Unwittingly, the activities of the serfs helped Alexander in his task. His accession prompted widespread rumours amongst the serfs that emancipation was imminent. Coupled to this was the feeling of those serfs who had been drafted into the army during the war, that its end would see them given their freedom. This was normal practice for those who left the army after a full period of service. When neither of these things happened, there was understandable disappointment and unrest.

Alexander addressed the problem in a roundabout way when he announced the peace treaty. He spoke of everyone enjoying 'the fruits of his honest labour, safeguarded by laws equally just and protective for all'. Some hoped that this finally signalled the end of serfdom. However, after years of unfulfilled hope, others were not a little cynical. The students of Kharkov, for example, parodied the Tsar's speech as follows:

1 We are grateful to you, dear Russians, for your blindness toward
all Our abuses. We are grateful to you, you veritable sheep, for
the patience with which you have borne all the disasters, all the
injustices, all the evil proceeding from Our despotic power . . .
5 We are grateful that you do not seek true enlightenment, but have
faith in Our slaves who fleece you . . . Sleep dear Russians as long
as We have not stolen your last shirt or shed the last drop of your
blood . . . Be assured that there has never been, nor will there
ever be, a single word of truth in Our promises of reform. Remain
10 forever exactly as you have always been. We are ineffably pleased
with you.

* Almost as if prompted by supporters of emancipation, the peasants
provided Alexander with another argument for change. The peasants
on the Black Sea coast revolted. They became convinced – on what
evidence it is not known – that Napoleon III had signed the treaty on
the express understanding that the serfs should be freed. It was further
rumoured that the Tsar was waiting at the small town of Perekop in the
Crimea to grant freedom to any who presented themselves to him.
Thousands set off to meet their 'little father'. Most were turned back at
gunpoint. Those who did reach the designated meeting place found
only disappointment.

Under previous Tsars these events would have normally led to
increased censorship and repression. However, Alexander wanted
change, if for no other reason than that he felt it to be his duty to ensure
that Russia was strong enough to defend herself. To prevent further
uncertainty, Alexander made the following speech to the Moscow
nobility, in March 1856.

1 . . . For the removal of certain unfounded reports I consider it
necessary to declare to you that I have not at present decided to
annihilate serfdom; but certainly, as you yourselves know, the
existing manner of possessing serfs cannot remain unchanged. It
5 is better to abolish serfdom from above than to await the time
when it will begin to abolish itself from below. I request you,
gentlemen, to consider how this can be put into execution, and to
submit my words to the nobility for their consideration . . .

* If Alexander hoped for some positive reaction from the nobility, he
was to be disappointed. The majority seemed to hope that this Tsar
would drop his plans, as his predecessors had done, if only they could
delay the decision for long enough. After continued pressure over the
next 18 months failed to make any real progress, Alexander finally
decided to force the issue. He instructed the Minister of the Interior to
produce a plan of action within a week. This plan was published in
November 1857. Each province was instructed to form a committee to

consider the proposals. Despite the reluctance of the majority, they did so as an Imperial Rescript (instruction) was not something which could easily be ignored.

In March 1859, the Tsar appointed 'drafting commissions' to examine the comments and proposals of the provincial committees. He appointed General Rostovstev, a close and trusted (if not particularly liberal) friend, to head the commissions. Rostovstev worked closely with the assistant Minister of the Interior, Milyutin, and the Slavophile, Samarin. Rostovstev was persuaded to support emancipation and organised the commissions in a way designed to favour those who wanted change. The proposals fell into two broad categories: those which supported reform and those which did not.

Sympathetic proposals came from 19 provinces. They generally supported emancipation and the distribution of some land to the peasants. In particular they favoured local rather than central administration of the reform. Predictably others were openly critical of reform and attacked Rostovstev and his colleagues for holding dangerously liberal views.

Representatives from the pro-reform provinces were invited to Moscow towards the end of 1859. They were seen in small groups, and gave their views orally. After these views had been considered, the opponents of reform were seen early in 1860. At this point Rostovstev died, and a known reactionary, Panin, was appointed in his place. Many saw this as a clear sign that conservative pressure on the Tsar was having the same effect as it had had on his predecessors. Although this pressure existed, it seems likely that Panin's appointment was an astute move to deflect it. Alexander continued to press strongly for reform. The drafting committees worked through the year. Some concessions were made to conservative feeling, but they were relatively minor. Under pressure from Alexander work was finished in October 1860. The Tsar supported the plans personally in the Council of State. This ensured their approval. The Emancipation Ukase (Decree) was published in February 1861. Despite the concessions it retained the spirit of the original proposal.

* The following extract from the Decree points to many of the underlying reasons behind Alexander's commitment to ending serfdom:

1 ... As the paternal character of the relations between the proprietors and the peasants became weakened, and, moreover, as the seigneural authority fell sometimes into hands exclusively occupied with their personal interests, those bonds of mutual
5 goodwill slackened, and a wide opening was made for an arbitrary sway, which weighed upon the peasants, was unfavourable to their welfare, and made them indifferent to all progress under the conditions of their existence . . .

We thus came to the conviction that the work of a serious
10 improvement of the condition of the peasants was a sacred
inheritance bequeathed to us by our ancestors, a mission which,
in the course of events, Divine providence called upon us to
fulfil . . .
   Having invoked the Divine assistance, we have resolved to
15 carry this work into execution.
   In virtue of the new dispositions . . . the peasants attached to
the soil will be invested within a term fixed by the law with all the
rights of free cultivators.

The Decree was long, complex and often obscure. It contained 17
articles and each article contained at least 100 sections. However, the
first article was clear: 'the right of bondage' was 'forever abolished'.
The serfs were to receive land from the estates of the nobility. In theory
they were to receive roughly the same amount of land they had
cultivated before emancipation. The State paid compensation to the
nobility, which was to be repaid by the peasants in the form of
'redemption payments'. The *mir* was established as the official organ of
self-government. The *mir* held the land collectively and it was collectively responsible for the payment ot taxes and redemption dues. It was
also responsible for administering justice via special courts. The serfs
were now free to enter trade or marry without permission, but they
were still subject to a separate system of justice from the rest of Russia.
   Emancipation was achieved at last, but there is often a gap between
theory and practice. This was just such a case. The complexities of the
Decree and the way in which it was to be implemented were to cause
many problems.

6   Results of Emancipation

After the enactment of a reform which they had sought for so long, one
might have expected jubilation from the serfs at least. But there was
little rejoicing. In the first four months after the Emancipation Decree,
there were 647 serious incidents of riot. In 1861 as a whole, there were
499 cases of riot which needed to be quelled by armed troops. Nor did
the peasants grow much fonder of the terms of the Decree as time
passed. That some landlords were far from content is to be expected, as
they lost land and serfs. But the bitter reaction from the peasants, who
received both freedom and land, needs explanation.
   * The single most important cause of this discontent was that the
peasants simply could not understand why they were being asked to pay
for land which their families had farmed for generations. As far as they
were concerned it was theirs by right. Many serfs genuinely believed
that the Tsar had never meant them to pay for what was so obviously
theirs, and that the local landowners were lying to them. The notion of

abstract property rights was something that was largely beyond their comprehension.

The situation did not improve as the details of land division were worked out, and the nature of the redemption payments became known. The division of land was decided at the local level, with the landlords, who were often in charge of the division, normally retaining the best land for themselves. To buy their land, the peasants had to make a 20 per cent initial payment, followed by 49 annual 'redemption payments'. These payments included an interest charge. This might have been feasible if the price fixed for the land had not so often been grossly inflated above its real worth. The following table shows how redemption costs varied according to area.

Area	Redemption Cost	Land value (Avg. 1863–72)
	(Millions of roubles)	
Black soil provinces	341	284
Non-black soil provinces	340	180
Western provinces	183	184

On average, serfs in the western provinces were charged a 'fair' price for the land they received. This was not true in other areas. In the worst cases, in the non-black soil provinces in the north, they were charged well over twice the land's actual value. Why were there such differences according to area?

The government was far from sympathetic to the Polish landlords in the western provinces, largely because they had long been a thorn in Russia's side with their demands for independence. The relatively few serfs in this area were therefore treated reasonably, as Russia did not have reason to support and protect the landlords who lived there. The significant differences appear in the other two areas. This was partly due to Alexander's wish not to alienate or unduly weaken the nobility, whom the Tsars had relied on for so long as a force for stability. In both these areas Alexander sought to protect the interests of the landlords as he saw them.

In the fertile black soil provinces many landlords were in favour of emancipation. There were two closely connected reasons for this. Firstly, if it could be used efficiently to provide grain for the growing export trade, the land was worth more than the serf's labour. Secondly, many landlords in this area felt that modern methods would lead to significantly increased profits. They wished to move to a system of wage labour in order to introduce these methods. The serfs in these provinces therefore had to pay only a small premium of 15 per cent to 20 per cent above the market value of the land they received. In the provinces to the north, however, the situation was very different. The land had never produced much above subsistence level in terms of food. The peasants had always depended on localised 'cottage industry' to supplement their incomes. The nobility relied heavily on 'rent' rather than labour (*barschina*) to provide their income. This 'rent' was often tied to the 'industrial' production of the serf rather than the value of the land. When it came to compensation for their loss therefore, it was not the value of the land that concerned the nobility so much as the loss of revenue. Thus the serfs found themselves paying almost double the actual value of the land they purchased.

These factors alone would have been enough to cause severe problems, but with modern farming methods and a new attitude to their relationship to the soil, the ex-serfs might still have overcome these difficulties. However, a group of essentially subsistence peasant farmers cannot be turned into modern agriculturalists at a stroke. Such modernisation required more than just ridding the serfs of their domination by the nobility. It required a radical change in the social and economic structure, and the attitude of the peasantry towards those structures. The Tsar was not in a position to implement or to offer such a change, even if the peasants had been willing and able to accept it.

The *mir* was not abolished. Indeed it was actually set up in places where it had not existed before, to provide uniformity and a very necessary stability at a time of rapid change. But the *mir* did not allow for the initiative and experiment which both Russia as a whole, and the peasantry, desperately needed. In economic terms it also often perpetuated many of the worst elements of pre-emancipation Russia. In many places the strip system continued, as did the three field system and periodic land redistribution. These practices positively discouraged innovation, improvement and progress.

The peasants were subject to the *mir*, and the special courts based on it. They were still outside the main body of law and functioned, for the most part, according to tradition and custom. The *mir* bound the peasants almost as firmly to their existing lifestyle as their former bondage had done. Where the *mir* had not existed before, its establishment was in some ways actually a backward step. The peasants may have become 'free', but they were still not the equal of other Russian citizens. They remained a class apart, subject to different laws and institutions which offered them fewer rights and less protection than other Russians. The nobility favoured the *mir* because it was collectively responsible for redemption payments. Many peasants favoured the *mir* because it appeared to offer collective security. The problem was that the more progressive elements of the peasantry often found it impossible to withdraw from the collective, thus severely limiting their options, and the collective nature of the *mir* helped to perpetuate old ideas and attitudes.

Coupled to these problems was the unfair distribution of land, not only in terms of quality, but also in terms of quantity. In European Russia the actual acreage held by ex-serfs only fell by about five per cent in the 15 years after 1861. However, in the best black soil provinces of the south, the holdings of ex-serfs fell by about 25 per cent. They also lost many customary rights to woodland and common pasture. This problem was exacerbated by the continuing and dangerously rapid growth in population, which had doubled between 1800 and 1860. Over the next 40 years it virtually redoubled. In 1858 the population was 68 million; by 1897 it was 125 million.

The standard response of the Russian peasant to the effects of population pressure was to seek more land. Although each individual peasant was free to buy and sell land – and this did take place – there was in a very real sense no more land to be had. The ability to buy and sell land had serious consequences. It led to an increase in the number of landless peasants, who often found it difficult to find alternative employment. It also led to increasing indebtedness amongst the many peasants who, although already in debt, borrowed more money to buy more land.

Yet another problem was that the Emancipation Decree did not come into effect across the country within the two years originally intended. The transitional period, in which ex-serfs still bore a 'temporary obligation' to their former masters, dragged on in many areas of Russia until December 1881, when transfer of lands was finally made compulsory.

Thus for a variety of reasons emancipation failed to transform the peasantry. Redemption payments were too high, the *mir* acted as a brake on innovation and new methods, the industrial base did not expand rapidly enough to attract the growing number of landless peasants, land was frequently apportioned unfairly and the whole process of land transfer dragged on over decades. The net result was that although productivity increased by perhaps 20 per cent by the end of the century, this was in effect yet another example of relative stagnation illustrated by the fact that agricultural productivity more than doubled in Japan during the same period.

* Emancipation had a far worse effect on the nobility. For the most part the nobility were totally unprepared for the rigours of existing in a competitive society, without serfs to rely on. Part of the reason for the generous compensation terms they received was that the government wished to ensure their survival as a moderating force in Russian society, in order to counteract more radical groups. However, emancipation failed to ensure the survival of the nobility. In fact, it hastened their demise. The extra money they received did little good. Half of the money received by the nobility in the first ten years after 1861 went to pay off existing debts. By 1905 the nobility had been forced to sell one third of the land they had kept in 1861. Of the land they still retained in 1905, over 50 per cent was mortgaged in some fashion. Though there were a few notable exceptions, particularly in the Ukraine and Georgia, a large proportion of the nobility simply could not make their estates

pay. They therefore declined steadily, as did their ability to act as a stabilising force in Russian society. The position and power of the nobility had been based on serfdom. Emancipation effectively condemned them as a class.

Perhaps the most important initial motivation for introducing emancipation was the desire to strengthen the Russian state – in military, economic and industrial terms. It was hoped that a revitalised peasant economy would provide the basis for industrialisation by providing surplus capital for investment. The combined effect of the failings examined above was that this aim was not achieved. Money was taken from the agricultural sector, but very little was put back in to encourage new methods and higher productivity. One can argue that agriculture was bled dry in order to finance industrialisation, but that the move was counterproductive in that the lack of investment in agriculture meant that it could not provide enough capital to finance effective industrialisation. Russia did of course make progress, but not when compared to the rapidly growing economies of western Europe. In comparative terms she was still falling further behind her competitors. New tensions were thus introduced into Russian society without achieving the central aim of the reform. The ramifications of this will be examined in later chapters.

7   Conclusion

Almost all historians agree that the Emancipation Decree was a momentous event in Russian history; that it was of great importance and that it failed to achieve its aims. However, there is considerable disagreement over the precise reasons for this failure. Part of the criticism of the terms of reform appears to have been generated by the search for causes of the 1917 revolution. That search has sometimes led to emancipation being assessed more in terms of Russia in 1917 than of Russia in 1861. In an attempt to find a 'convenient' cause of the momentous events of 1917, it seems that some historians may have been overly eager to lay the blame for the revolution, at least partly, on the shortcomings of emancipation.

Pipes (see Further Reading) characterises emancipation as being too cautious, too little and too late. With the benefit of hindsight, it is possible to have sympathy with this argument in terms of Russian history in general. But a consideration of the problems faced by Alexander seems to suggest that it is a little unfair to him. Previous Tsars could certainly have been more determined in their attempts to modernise Russia, but Alexander could hardly have acted with greater speed. If we dismiss the idea of 'too late' in terms of Alexander on the basis that he could hardly have acted sooner, we are left with 'too cautious' and 'too little'.

There is no doubt that 'redemption payments' were too heavy for the majority of ex-serfs to bear. But Alexander could hardly have been expected to destroy the nobility deliberately. He wanted and felt he needed them as a stabilising conservative influence in post-emancipation Russia. It is clear that the lack of full civil rights and the continuance of the *mir* proved to be significant blocks to progress. Yet what was the alternative? The nobility were clearly not appropriate people to continue the administration of the peasants. The administration itself was notorious for its corruption. Indeed, one of the chief complaints of the state peasants was the corruption of the local officials. A modern democratic alternative was certainly not on offer. So it would seem that allowing the peasants to run their own affairs at this time via a traditional, popular and trusted institution was a reasonable course of action.

The key to understanding the effects and success/failure of emancipation is to see them in the context of the other problems facing Russia. These problems may have been overcome if the Tsar had been prepared to abandon autocracy, but he was not. As Alexander emphasised in 1865 over another area of reform, he still believed firmly in the principle of autocracy. He still believed that he derived power from 'God Himself'. As with Alexander I before him, Alexander II found it difficult to be a reforming autocrat. His basic motivation was to make Russia strong and serve his people, not to be a liberal reformer. He did not believe that Russia would benefit from liberal reforms – and, of course, it would be simplistic to condemn Alexander for this stance. In political, social and economic terms, Russia in 1861 was still a backward nation. There is every reason to suppose that had any more radical reform been imposed from above, the Russian state would have collapsed into anarchy and chaos. The fact that emancipation still left the Empire far behind much of Europe should not obscure the very real and very dramatic impact it had on contemporary Russia.

No such attempt at change, even one backed by an imperial decree, can transform any large society at a stroke. Even if one does not consider emancipation, Alexander did bring about a surprising, indeed an almost revolutionary degree of reform and change (see pages 72–85). The outcome of emancipation depended, to a large degree, on these other reforms. They were necessarily dependent on each other for their success or failure. The next two chapters will consider the nature and impact of these other areas of reform. If they had been more successful, emancipation, with all its faults, might also have been more successful.

Summary – The Emancipation of the Serfs

Making notes on 'The Emancipation of the Serfs'

Your notes on this chapter should give you an understanding of the long and short-term causes of emancipation. You should also have a basis from which you can discuss the reasons for the apparent failure of emancipation to fulfil the expectations of different groups. Pay close attention to the political, social and economic elements in both cases.

The following headings and subheadings should be of help in making your notes:

1.   Alexander II
2.   The Crimean Effect
2.1. The impact of the war
3.   Why Emancipation of the Serfs?
3.1. Importance of the serfs
3.2. The failure of serfdom for:
     The serfs
     The landlords
     The economy
3.3. Alexander's reaction
4.   The Condition of the Peasantry
4.1. State peasants
4.2. The serfs
4.3. Types of serfdom
4.4. Why was there no emancipation before?
5.   The Road to Emancipation
5.1. Emancipation proposed
5.2. Reactions
5.3. Drafting commissions
5.4. Terms of the Decree
6.   Results of Emancipation
6.1. Negative reactions
6.2. Drawbacks to emancipation for:
     The serfs
     The nobility
     The economy
7.   Conclusion
7.1. Causes of failure
7.2. Positive aspects

Answering essay questions on 'The Emancipation of the Serfs'

You may need to use much of the information in this chapter to answer the more general questions on Alexander's reforms discussed on page 87. You are also likely to be asked to answer specific questions on emancipation. These questions will concentrate on causes, consequences, or both.

An example of the first type of question would be:

1 'Why did emancipation take place in Russia in 1861?'

The question is a straightforward 'Why?' Plan your answer by following these steps:

a)   Make a list of about six reasons why emancipation took place in 1861 – for example – Because Alexander wanted to strengthen Russia (make sure that you explain the ways in which he wanted to strengthen Russia).
b)   List the evidence you would use to back up your statements.
c)   Decide on their order of importance.

Be careful how you decide on their order of importance. Would the order be different for example if the question was:

2   'Why did Alexander II emancipate the serfs in 1861?' or
3   'Why was the Crimean War followed by emancipation?'

How would you alter your choice of reasons or their use for these two questions? Remember also that history is about the unique and the particular. You could and should add depth to your answer to any of these questions by devoting at least a paragraph to why emancipation had not taken place before.

The second type of question might be:

4   'What were the consequences of emancipation during the reign of Alexander II?'

Emancipation is normally taken to be a relative failure. Here you could again repeat the exercise above and list the major ways in which it did fail, with evidence to illustrate the nature and importance of failure in the areas you choose. Again however, remember to avoid a completely one-sided approach. There are nearly always two sides to an argument. Include at least some reference to the positive aspects of emancipation. You should return to this question after reading Chapters 6 and 7, to decide what information on other aspects of Alexander's reign might usefully be included.

An example of the combined question would be:

5.   'Why, and with what results during his reign, did Alexander II emancipate the serfs in Russia?'

Source-based questions on 'The Emancipation of the Serfs'

1   Serfdom – a Russian view
Carefully read the extract from Vodovosova's memoirs on pages 57–8. Answer the following questions:
a)   What does this extract tell us about the control the landlords had over the lives of the serfs? (2 marks)

b)   How did the serfs take revenge on the Tonchevs? Why did they adopt this particular approach? (3 marks)
c)   What would you want to know about the author in deciding how credible her evidence is? (3 marks)
d)   What are the dangers of generalising from evidence such as this? (2 marks)

2   Serfdom – a foreign view

Carefully read the extract from the British traveller on page 58. Answer the following questions:
a)   In what ways does this picture of the serf's life differ from that given in the previous extract? (3 marks)
b)   Do these differences mean that one of the extracts is inaccurate? Justify your answer fully. (3 marks)
c)   What does the final sentence tell you about the perspective of this author? Does this perspective lessen the value of this extract as evidence about serfdom? (4 marks)

3   Kharkov students 1856

Carefully read the extract from the Kharkov students on page 60. Answer the following questions:
a)   Why do we not know the identity of the authors of this piece? (2 marks)
b)   What is the general tone of this piece? Does it expect the Tsar's promises to be fulfilled? (4 marks)
c)   What words or phrases clearly point to the bias of this extract? (4 marks)

4   Alexander's speech – March 1856

Carefully read the extract from the Tsar's speech on page 60. Answer the following questions:
a)   What is the stated purpose of this speech? Does Alexander have other reasons for publishing it? Is it, for example, intended for two different audiences? (6 marks)
b)   Give examples of Alexander trying (i) to ingratiate himself with, and (ii) to threaten his audience. (2 marks)
c)   What is the underlying meaning of 'request' in line 6? (2 marks)

5   The Emancipation Decree

Carefully read the extract from the Emancipation Decree on pages 61–2. Answer the following questions:
a)   What reasons are given for emancipation? (4 marks)
b)   What means of persuasion does the Tsar employ? (4 marks)
c)   What other reasons, not mentioned in the extract, did Alexander have for supporting emancipation? (4 marks)

d)   What explanations can you offer for Alexander not including these other reasons? (5 marks)

6   Gambling for souls

Carefully study the cartoon reproduced on page 54. Answer the following questions:

a)   Identify (by type rather than by name) (i) the people bound together and lying on the table, and (ii) the card players. (2 marks)

b)   What message is the artist attempting to communicate? (2 marks)

c)   Comment on the techniques used by the artist to put over his point of view. Concentrate especially on the situation he has chosen to illustrate and the way in which the card players and spectators are portrayed. (6 marks)

CHAPTER 5

The Reforming Tsar

1 Motivation

Serfdom had in many ways been the cornerstone of autocratic Russia. After emancipation, the issue was not whether there would be other reforms, but rather how they would be planned and implemented. Alexander was convinced that in order to maintain stability and achieve his aim of a strong Russian state, he needed to transform much of the existing social and political system. He pushed through reforms in almost all areas of life: local government, the legal system, the military, education, censorship and the economy. Without the strong personal pressure he exerted in favour of reform, much of it would not have taken place.

2 Local Government

The development of local government clearly characterises Alexander's attitude to reform. At his accession there was effectively no elected local government. He felt that this contributed significantly to administrative inefficiency. Alexander was therefore determined to bring in a measure of local government, but he was equally determined that it should not appear that it was being forced upon him. He firmly suppressed public calls for reform.

In 1859, whilst discussing the terms of emancipation, nobles from the Tver province went too far in Alexander's eyes. They called for an independent judiciary, some form of local government independent of the bureaucracy, and an elected body to deal with economic affairs. Their spokesman, Unkovsky, was promptly sent into exile. In 1862, 13 nobles from Tver called for an elected and classless national assembly. They were imprisoned in St Petersburg. Alexander was not prepared to countenance a national assembly, nor open debate on the matter.

However, he was determined that reform of local government would take place. The commission which he had set up in 1861 had still produced no firm proposals towards the end of 1863. In November, he therefore instructed the commission to finish its task by the end of the year. The decree establishing the *zemstva* was duly published in January 1864.

* The *zemstva* were local elected councils. The powers given to them reflect the nature of the struggle which was taking place between the liberals and the more reactionary elements in Russia. The liberals wanted the *zemstva* to have real power and in part they succeeded. The *zemstva* were given responsibility for public education, public health, local economic development, road building and provision of services

such as water and fire prevention. The liberals also wanted them to be given power over the disposal of imperial taxes, but in this they failed. This failure shows the dichotomy which existed between the desire for reform and the equally strong desire to maintain autocratic control. The argument was clearly put by Valuev, the conservative Minister of the Interior appointed in 1861. He stated that:

1 To give the *zemstva* a voice in matters common to the whole empire would be to break up the unitary executive power of the empire and distribute it among some forty or fifty bodies. This would expose the social order and the entire imperial structure to
5 perils which must be apparent to everyone.

Alexander wanted reform, he wanted to devolve some power from the centre, but he also wished to remain in firm control and to maintain stability. It was felt that giving the *zemstva* control over imperial finance would undermine those aims.

The membership of the *zemstva* also reflected the desire of the conservative elements and the Tsar to retain the nobility as a bulwark against undue radicalism. The *zemstva* were two-tiered: district (*uezd*) and provincial (*gubernia*). The seats for the district *zemstva* were divided amongst the three classes: 45 per cent to the nobility; 40 per cent to the peasants and 15 per cent to the townsmen and the clergy. The district *zemstva* then elected representatives to the provincial level. The system was designed to ensure that no one grouping had overall control. At the local level this succeeded, but it is easy to see why the nobility tended to dominate at the provincial level.

The *zemstva* did not treat all groups equally. Local taxation continued to favour the nobility rather than the peasantry, but by virtue of their local knowledge, the *zemstva* did improve local administration in the areas in which they were allowed to operate. The following comments written by Sir Mackenzie Wallace, who lived in Russia from 1870 to 1875, is representative of the 'objective' assessments which have come down to us.

1 What surprised me most in this [*zemstvo*] assembly was that it was comprised partly of nobles and partly of peasants . . . and that no trace of antagonism seemed to exist between the two classes. Landed proprietors and their cidevant serfs, emancipated only
5 ten years before, evidently met for the moment on a footing of equality. The discussions were carried on chiefly by the nobles, but on more than one occasion peasant members rose to speak, and their remarks, always clear, practical, and to the point, were invariably listened to with respectful attention . . .
10 The *zemstvo* . . . fulfils tolerably well without scandalous speculation and jobbery, its commonplace, every-day duties . . .

It has done a very great deal to provide medical aid and primary education for the common people, and it has improved wonderfully the condition of hospitals, lunatic asylums, and other
15 benevolent institutions committed to its charge. In its efforts to aid the peasantry it has helped to improve the native breeds of horses and cattle, and it has created a system of obligatory fire insurance, together with means for preventing and extinguishing fires in the villages – a most important matter in a country where
20 the peasants live in wooden houses and big fires are fearfully frequent.

In 1870, a Municipal Statute set up a similar system in the towns. A town council (*duma*) was elected by Russian male property holders over the age of 25. They too were given responsibility for public health, provision of services, roads, public education and local trade and industry. The one key area they were not given control over was the police. This was an area over which the imperial government wished to and did keep firm control.

It has been argued, both by historians and contemporary critics, that the success of the *zemstva* showed how capable the 'people' were of looking after themselves, and that it was shortsighted and indeed tragic that the representative principle was not extended to central government. There is merit in this argument, but it should not lessen appreciation of the significance of the establishment of the *zemstva*. At the local level at least, representation was now much broader than in many supposedly advanced western countries.

3 Legal Reform

Almost certainly of equal importance was the judicial reform introduced in 1864. The Russian judicial system was sorely in need of reform. There were numerous different types of court and officials were often ill-trained and illiterate. Evidence was normally written, the accused rarely saw the judges, and the written evidence of the nobility was usually given more credence than that from any other group. Graft was rife and cases often dragged on for years, as vividly expressed in the proverb: 'No grease, no motion'.

The reform of 1864 was intended to sweep away all the old abuses and to set up a system which was not only fair and just, but was seen to be so. As the Tsar himself put it in his decree to the senate:

1 On ascending to the throne of my ancestors, one of my first wishes publicly proclaimed in the manifesto of 19 March 1856, was: 'May justice and mercy reign in our courts!' Ever since that time, amidst other reforms called for by the needs of our national
5 life, I have never ceased to reflect on the manner of achieving this

object through a better organisation of the judiciary . . .

    [These statutes are intended] . . . to establish in Russia expeditious, just, merciful, and impartial courts for all our subjects; to raise the judicial authority by giving it proper independence and,
10 in general, to increase in the people that respect for the law which national well-being requires, and which must be the constant guide of all and everyone from the highest to the lowest.

This is almost exactly what the reform did. To avoid bribery, salaries were set deliberately high. Trials became public, trial by jury was introduced and appeal courts were set up. It was now expected that oral evidence would be presented and cross-examined in open court. There were two tiers to the system. Justices of the Peace were elected by the district *zemstva* for a period of three years. Judges were nominated to the regular courts by the Tsar. Once they were appointed they were virtually guaranteed independence as it was very difficult to remove them.

    * Wallace was in no doubt as to the effectiveness of the new system. He stated that:

1 In the Justice of Peace Courts . . . the Justice, always scrupulously polite without the distinction of persons, listened patiently to the complaint, tried to arrange the affair amicably, and when his efforts failed, gave his decision at once according to the law and
5 common sense. No attention was paid to rank or social position . . . No wonder such courts became popular among the masses; and their popularity increased when it became known that the affairs were disposed of expeditiously, without unnecessary formalities and without any bribes or blackmail.

It might seem that this is too rosy a picture to believe. However, if further evidence is needed that the judiciary and the juries took seriously their freedom to operate, one has only to examine the Vera Zasulich case in 1878 (see page 95). In this case, an admitted revolutionary who had shot General Trepov was found not guilty against all the evidence and the express wishes of the Minister of Justice.

    Of course, this case points to some idiosyncrasies in the system. Firstly, the authorities could still use powers of administrative arrest and special courts for certain crimes. After the Zasulich case the authorities never again relied on the regular courts to deal with terrorist activity. It also points to the fact that juries often acted as they felt it right to act, rather than as the evidence suggested they should. There were set sentences for certain crimes, but juries found a way round this restriction. In more than one case it is recorded that juries, upon being asked: 'Do you find the accused guilty to the charge of horse-stealing?'

replied firmly: 'Yes, the accused is found guilty of stealing rabbits.'
Thus the jury reduced the severity of the sentence whilst admitting the
guilt of the accused. Nor was this attitude restricted to the juries.
Wallace records that the Justices often carried their sense of duty to
what might to us appear to be extremes.

> 1 Imagining that their mission was to eradicate the conceptions and
>   habits of serfage, they sometimes used their authority for giving
>   lessons in philanthropic liberalism, and took a malicious delight
>   in wounding the susceptibilities, and occasionally even the mate-
> 5 rial interests, of those whom they regarded as enemies of the good
>   cause.

Such cases were not that common. They became less so as it was
realised that the judiciary was by and large independent and fair.
Attempts to misuse the system deliberately declined rapidly, while the
efficiency of the courts rose dramatically. Three times as many cases as
the authorities had anticipated were heard. The courts became trusted
and gained the confidence and respect of all social groups – except
perhaps the conservative élite.

There was one consequence which had not been anticipated. Open
and efficient courts needed trained lawyers and judges. The Tsar agreed
to the setting up of an independent bar. This led to the growth of a
body of people, trained in the art of persuasion, fully conversant with
officialdom and the law, and generally disposed towards liberal ideas.
Such a body required freedom to debate and discuss ideas. It was to
prove the ideal breeding ground for reformers, some of whom were to
become prominent revolutionaries in the future. The creation of this
'dangerous' group was not the intention of the judicial reforms, but it
was a necessary by-product.

4 Military Reform

The Crimean War had shown all too clearly the shortcomings of the
military system. Despite the fact that the army consumed almost one
third of the government's income, it had failed to defeat inferior
numbers of foreign troops on Russian territory. Though this was partly
due to problems of transportation, it also pointed to other serious
problems.

The command structure and the administration were inflexible and
inefficient. Punishment was often severe and barbaric. The period of
service for conscripts was 25 years and often viewed as a life sentence,
and those who could do so avoided military service in any way they
could. To make matters worse the parade ground was normally given
greater priority than the ability to fight.

In 1861 the Tsar appointed Miliutin as Minister of War, with the explicit task of reforming the military. Miliutin held office for the next 20 years. He was an able administrator who took a keen interest in all affairs of state and generally took a liberal stance on most issues. Though often strongly opposed by conservative elements in the government and the army, he enjoyed the enthusiastic support of the Grand Duke Constantine, the Minister of the Marine. This imperial support often helped him through turbulent waters.

Miliutin sought to humanise the military and improve its efficiency in all aspects. He set about his task with considerable vigour. In 1862, regional commands were set up in four areas. The aim was to improve efficiency by decentralising administration and supply. In 1864, six further regional commands were established. In 1863 the more extreme forms of corporal punishment were ended and the Military Code was revised. Miliutin also set about reducing the influence of the old cadet corps, which until now had produced the officers of the army. He set up special army schools (*Junker* schools) which were open to all. This was a significant step forward, and by 1871 twelve per cent of the *Junker* students were not from the nobility. This was an important advance away from privilege and patronage, and towards promotion and selection on merit. The compulsory length of service for conscripts had already been reduced from 25 to 16 years in 1859. Plans were laid to further reduce the length of, and to extend the liability to, service. This was intended to make the army a less fearsome prospect and to prevent people avoiding military service.

As might be expected, these reforms generated a good deal of antagonism amongst the traditionalists in the army and amongst the conservative elements in the government. The nobility, reeling from the shock of the numerous reforms which were undermining their rights and position, closed ranks against the idea that their sons should be treated equally with the sons of their former serfs. It began to look as if they would prevent Miliutin's plans for further reform from being put into practice. However, the striking success of the Prussian army against the French in 1870–1 gave Miliutin the lever he needed. It showed what could be achieved by a modern army which was efficiently organised and led. Using the Prussian example as a model, he was able to force his reforms through.

In 1874, the Manifesto and Statute on Universal Military Service was published. It became law in 1875. Liability to military service and conscription was extended to all classes. The hiring of substitute conscripts was forbidden. Service in the army was no longer an optional punishment for criminals. All males upon reaching 21 years of age had to register. About one quarter of these were chosen by lot to serve. Only those unfit for service were exempted – though in practice deferments on compassionate grounds were obtainable for all classes. Service was limited to 15 years, of which normally only about seven years would be spent on active service. Length of service was significantly reduced for those who volunteered and for those with an education. University graduates, for example, only had to serve six months with the colours. Even those with merely a primary education had to serve only four years. Though these reductions in service obviously favoured the educated (and therefore the nobility and the rich over the peasantry) it was still a major step forward in social as well as military terms. In the area of conscription at least, the son of the lowest peasant was now theoretically treated in exactly the same manner as the son of the highest noble.

This change was not inevitable. Miliutin's diary provides a clear and fascinating insight into the bitter infighting which went on throughout 1873. Indeed as the year drew to a close, he seemed closer to despair than to one about to reach a cherished goal.

1 December 31, 1873. On the last day of the year my thoughts turn back and quickly run through a whole series of impressions preserved in my memory. For me the year 1873 passed by as a dark shadow; it leaves behind none but melancholy impressions.
5 Not in a single preceding year have I endured so much unpleasantness, sorrow and failure. The intrigue against me, begun long since, has fully matured and has broken out in all its vileness. My enemies have not succeeded in fully attaining their aims; they cannot consider themselves victorious but have
10 nonetheless managed to injure me in the eyes of the sovereign and to make my position within the government almost impossible. Seeing at every step disaffection and mistrust on the part of the person whose will decides all matters finally and without appeal, I am paralysed in my activity. . . . By now it is impossible for me to
15 direct the organisation of military affairs with the independence and energy with which I have been directing them for over twelve years. As for general affairs of state which lie outside the sphere of the military department, in this respect I have been entirely set aside. Everything is done under the sole influence of Count
20 Shuvalov [Head of the Third Section from 1866 to 1874], who has alarmed the sovereign by his daily reports on the fearful dangers to which both the state and the sovereign are said to be exposed. All Shuvalov's power rests upon this bugbear. On the pretext of protecting the person of the sovereign and the monarchy, Count
25 Shuvalov interferes in matters of every kind, and questions of every kind are decided on the basis of his tale bearing. He has surrounded the sovereign with his own supporters; all new appointments are made in accordance with his directions. In this way, by now the majority of members in the Committee of
30 Ministers always act in unison with Count Shuvalov, the way an orchestra follows the baton of its conductor. Timashev, Count

Tolstoy, Count Palen, Valuev – all are obedient tools of Count Shuvalov . . .

There can be little doubt that in the face of such opposition only the support of the Tsar could have enabled Miliutin to force his reform through. Alexander put his full weight behind enabling Miliutin to do so. He felt strongly that the defence of 'the fatherland' was and should be a common concern to all his subjects. He saw it as his 'sacred task', and the 'sacred task' of all Russians, to ensure that Russia was able to defend herself. Put in these terms, there were few who dared oppose his view.

In some senses one can argue that this reform was the most 'democratic' in its implications of all the reforms carried out under Alexander II. It treated all Russians equally, excepting the reference to education. However, it was not a complete success. The General Staff, although improved, were still burdened with far too many regulations and diverse tasks. Not until 1900 was it finally agreed that their duties should be clearly laid down – even then this had not come into operation before the Russo-Japanese War began in 1904. Army doctors could still be bribed to declare people unfit for service. The quality of training and leadership still lagged far behind that of the Prussians. Yet great improvements were made, and their effects could clearly be seen in the improved performance of the army in the Russo-Turkish War of 1878.

5   Education

Education is a recurrent problem for autocratic regimes. How can they educate people without at the same time encouraging them to think and question? Perhaps the simple answer is that it cannot be done. Until 1861 strict and repressive control was maintained over education. Then the Tsar appointed Golvonin as Minister of Education. Golvonin, like Miliutin, was a close colleague of Grand Duke Constantine and was most definitely aligned with the liberal reformers.

Golvonin set out at once to reform the education system. It was decided to develop primary education in the villages. The task was soon handed over to the *zemstva*. The *duma* later carried out a similar task in the towns. Both were encouraged to expand primary education. Between 1861 and 1881 the number of primary and secondary schools increased fourfold. In 1862 new schools were placed under the jurisdiction of the Ministry of Education rather than under the control of the Church. This was intended to free them of the traditionally stifling influence of the Church. New schemes of work were developed and prizes were offered for the best textbooks produced. Significant progress was made in terms of both the quality of the education provided and pupil numbers.

The University Regulations of 1863 were Golvonin's most famous contribution to the education system, although perhaps they were of no greater impact than his work with primary and secondary schools. These regulations changed the basis of university activity. They allowed a freedom of expression which had certainly not been seen for 50 years. The universities were given virtual autonomy in administrative matters and, although the curriculum was prescribed by the Ministry, much greater freedom was allowed in terms of presentation and treatment. Rectors were appointed for four years by a Council of Professors. Deans were elected by faculties for three years. The teaching of law was upgraded, and in the case of constitutional law was actually reinstated. This was a major change. However, perhaps the most far-reaching of the regulations are set out below. They point to a radical change in stance and attitude towards the liberty and needs of both the individual and the group within Russian society.

The University Regulations of 18 June 1863

90.   Besides students, outsiders are also permitted to attend lectures . . .

107.   For the relief of needy students, the Universities are allowed to grant deferments of payment, or to reduce it by as much as one-half, or even to waive it entirely . . .

114.   Academic degrees may be obtained both by Russian subjects and by foreigners . . .

129.   Universities are accorded the right to import, at liberty and duty free, scholarly texts of any kind from abroad . . .

130.   Books, manuscripts, and periodical publications that the universities receive from foreign countries are not subject to examination by the censorship.

Alexander took a close personal interest in the drafting of the Regulations and in the promotion of the universities. Scholarships were set up to support the best students. Fact-finding expeditions abroad were encouraged. The universities began to flourish in the new atmosphere of open enquiry.

* An incident in 1866 prevented this atmosphere from continuing to develop unchecked. A former student of Kazan University attempted to assassinate the Tsar. This was the excuse Golvonin's opponents had sought. A commission appointed to investigate the attempt attributed it to the growth of radical ideas fostered by the newly relaxed and liberal education policies. Golvonin was replaced by the much more conservative Dmitri Tolstoy. Although Tolstoy restricted entry to the universities somewhat, and placed some disciplinary powers in the hands of the police rather than the university authorities, he did not seriously interfere with the foundation laid down by Golvonin. The universities continued to flourish until the end of Alexander's reign.

However, Tolstoy's impact was greater in other areas. In 1871 he introduced a new 'classical' curriculum into the *gymnasia* (higher secondary schools). Great emphasis was placed on the study of Greek, Latin and mathematics. The same law also gave power to the Ministry to dictate curricula in schools and to control appointments, as well as making graduation considerably more dependent upon rote learning. In 1872 Tolstoy took similar powers over the modern technical schools (*realschule*), whilst at the same time increasing their number. He also made it a condition of entry to the universities that students had graduated from a *gymnasium*. At the same time new technical institutes were set up for students from the *realschule*. This meant that they could continue their studies without being exposed to the possibly corrupting influence of the universities.

Russian liberals saw these measures as unreservedly reactionary in nature, designed merely to prevent the spread of modern knowledge. This feeling was doubtless strengthened by Tolstoy's close links with the Orthodox Church. Nevertheless, students from district schools were enabled to go on to *gymnasia*. Though the intent of the reforms may have been repressive, the actual effect was not that severe. Indeed there were positive aspects in terms of administrative efficiency and equality of opportunity. Positive steps were also made in other areas, albeit without Tolstoy's active support. Women's education made great strides. 1872 saw Moscow University organise the first courses for women. Women were also admitted to the Medical Academy in St Petersburg. After an Imperial Statute in 1876, five universities set up degree courses for women. By 1881 there were some 2000 women studying at universities in Russia.

Again, therefore, we see an uneasy balance being struck between progressive liberal initiatives and a desire to maintain control of events. The Tsar first appointed a liberal, Golvonin, to bring in radical changes to the educational system. Once these initiatives were firmly in place (and admittedly under pressure from conservative advisers) he appointed a conservative figure, Tolstoy, to keep the effects of these changes in check. However he did not allow Tolstoy actually to undo Golvonin's work. Then and now, critics have argued that this merely gave the Tsar and Russia the worst of all worlds, and that what was needed was continuing and thoroughgoing reform. But the Tsar did not want revolution. He felt that it was his duty to maintain his position. As we shall see below, he had every reason to beware. More change had been thrust upon Russia in ten years than had taken place in the previous 150 years. The results were bound to be somewhat unsettling. He was determined not to allow the situation to develop to the point where it could no longer be controlled.

6 Censorship

As seen above (pages 43–6), the censorship laws under Nicholas were extremely complex, and could be very harsh. After Alexander's accession the situation relaxed for a time, but when, in 1863, responsibility for censorship was passed to Valuev, the Minister of the Interior, the system again became tighter. The duality of the Tsar's approach to reform is shown by the fact that once censorship had been tightened, the relatively progressive Press Laws were published in 1865. Some of the key elements of these laws are given below:

1   I. Freed from preliminary censorship are:
    A. In both capitals:
    1. All currently issued periodical publications, if their publishers shall themselves state this desire.
5   2. All original writings of not less than 160 printed pages in length.
    B. Everywhere:
    1. All government publications.
    2. All publications of academics, universities, and
10   learned societies and institutions.
    3. All publications in the ancient classical languages and translations from those languages.
    4. Sketches, diagrams and maps.
    . . .
15 IV. Everyone who wishes to issue a new periodical publication in the form of a newspaper, magazine or anthology is obliged, now as before, to obtain permission of the minister of internal affairs.
    . . .
20 XXVIII. The minister of internal affairs is accorded the right to issue warnings to periodical publications, indicating the articles giving cause for this. A third warning suspends publication for a period of time designated by the minister . . . but not exceeding six months . . .
25   . . .
  XXX. If the minister . . . deems it necessary . . . to prohibit the publication altogether . . . he is to make representation to the First Department of the Governing Senate.

Although the detested preliminary censorship was largely abolished, the statute retained teeth with which to work. Critics argue that censorship remained strict. It is true that several papers received warnings within the first few weeks. It is also true that in 1866 the radical journal *The Contemporary* was prohibited. However, the former seems to have been by nature of a warning not to go too far, and the latter occurred in the wake of the attempt on the Tsar's life. Censorship was strict by modern British standards, but in comparison to what had gone before in Russia it represented a considerable increase in freedom of both ideas and expression. The number of new books which were published per year doubled between 1855 and 1864, and trebled between 1864 and 1881. It was not until the last few years of Alexander's reign that censorship really began to bite hard again, and even then it was not nearly as severe as it had been under Nicholas I. There was a change in the relationship between publisher and censor – a mood of cooperation rather than repression prevailed.

7   Economic Progress

Reutern was appointed Minister of Finance in 1862, and continued in office until 1878. He created a unified Treasury and introduced an efficient centralised administrative system. After 1862 budgets were published, and in 1863 a system of excise duties replaced the medieval system of farming out licenses to sell certain goods, especially spirits, which were still a key source of revenue. He modernised and stream-lined the fiscal organisation of the state.

Of greater importance were the moves to stimulate the Russian economy. A great deal of effort was expended on establishing a railway network. When Alexander II came to the throne there were less than 700 miles of track laid. By 1881, there were over 14,000 miles of track. This was achieved by initially guaranteeing the annual dividend on shares of investors, especially those from abroad who were uncertain as to the reliability of the investment. Much of the new railway system was designed to encourage grain exports, which were Russia's chief source of foreign revenue. This was a great success. In 1864, exports stood at approximately 26 million tons. By 1880 they had risen to 86 million tons.

Of almost equal importance was the effort made to develop and expand Russia's financial institutions. In 1855 the majority of Russians still relied on moneylenders to service their needs. By 1878 there were 278 municipal banks, 727 loan and savings associations, 566 joint-stock companies and 33 joint-stock commercial banks. Much of this explo-sion was the result of Reutern's sound administration and encourage-ment. Russian industry had long suffered from the fact that it was very difficult to raise money for investment and expansion. This growth of the financial institutions did not solve the problem, but it did much to alleviate it.

* Virtually nothing was ignored which might assist economic expan-sion. Jews in Russia had lived under strict rules about what trade they could practice and where they could live. Up to 1855 they were restricted to living in the border regions – 'the Pale of Settlement'. It was realised that these restrictions meant that the Jews could not make a full contribution to the Russian economy. Under Alexander II, many

of the more onerous restrictions were lifted. In 1859 Jewish merchants of the First Guild (those who paid above a certain amount in taxes) and all foreign Jews were allowed to live and trade throughout the Empire. In 1860 this right was extended to all Jews who had served in certain regiments, and in 1867 to all Jews who had been soldiers. Perhaps the most important move, and certainly the most significant was the *Policy on Jewish Artisans* issued in 1865. This law abolished the 'pale' for Jewish artisans.

1 Jewish mechanics, distillers, brewers, and masters [craftsmen] and artisans in general are permitted to reside, in conformity with their passports and permits, anywhere outside the pale designated for the permanent settlement of Jews . . .

The importance of this move lies in the motivation behind it. Anti-semitism still prevailed. Indeed some forms of restrictive legislation (the closing of many Jewish schools and the limiting of Jewish representation) increased after 1863. So, the motivation lay for the most part not in any view of what was right and just, but in what made good economic sense. This is clearly shown by the following note from the Minister of the Interior to the Tsar in 1865.

1 The reason for the decline of the handicraft industry among the Jews must be sought in the general limitations upon the civil rights of this people . . . and most of all in the prohibition upon Jewish residence outside the regions designated for their settle-
5 ment.
　　From information in the possession of Internal Affairs it is clear that those who suffer most from this limitation on the rights of Jews to live outside the pale . . . are the artisans, Christian as well as Jewish . . .
10　In keeping with these convictions the Ministry of Internal Affairs considers that Jewish artisans should immediately be accorded the opportunity to reside outside their pale of settlement. There is no doubt that such permission would be advantageous in every respect.

* As with the other areas discussed in this chapter and with emancipation, the results, whatever the motive, were considerable compared to what had gone before. Progress was not always smooth as there were many complex interacting forces at work, but progress there most certainly was. One might be forgiven for expecting, as Alexander almost certainly did, that public reactions would be favourable. In general terms initial reactions were usually supportive. But the reaction of the intelligentsia was far from favourable. This was important because the intelligentsia were the opinion leaders of their day, and their views were beginning to count. We must now examine the reasons for this apparently strange response.

1859	Length of service in army reduced
1863	Corporal punishment restricted
1864	The *Zemstvo* established New army schools established The judicial reforms
1874	Universal military service introduced
1876	Women admitted to universities

Summary – The Reforming Tsar

Making notes on 'The Reforming Tsar'

The key points to look for in this chapter are:

What was changed?
What were the effects of change?
Why was it changed?
What prevented further change?
What was left unchanged?

The following headings should help you to include the main points:

1.   The Tsar's Motivation
2.   Local Government
2.1. Maintaining control
2.2. The *zemstva*: powers; successes; limitations
3.   Legal Reform
3.1. Nature of the reform
3.2. The reform in practice
4.   Military Reform
4.1. The army
5.   Education
5.1. Golvonin
5.2. Tolstoy
5.3. Checks and balances

6. Censorship
7. The Economy
7.1. Reutern's reforms
7.2. The Jewish question

Answering essay questions on 'The Reforming Tsar'

You will need to use the information in this chapter together with the information in the last chapter to answer general questions on Alexander's domestic policy. Carefully consider the following questions:

1. 'Why did Alexander II introduce so much reform?'
2. 'Whose needs were met by the reforms of Alexander II?'
3. 'How far were the domestic reforms of Alexander II mere "window dressing by a Tsar whose main intention was to prevent more radical change"?'

The first question is relatively straightforward. If you make a list of each of Alexander's reforms and then note down against each reform what problems they aimed to solve and what they aimed to achieve, you have the basis of the essay. However, it is not quite that simple. You need to discuss at least briefly the idea that he did not bring in real reform. Indeed you could argue, as some historians have done, that none of his reforms were intended to do anything else other than maintain the existing social order. Yet this is a very difficult task and you might be well advised to stick to a more 'normal' approach to the question.

The second question is more difficult. It not only asks whose needs the reforms were intended to meet, it also means that you should examine what groups might have been unintentionally satisfied or not satisfied by reform. When you have established the groups on which you are going to concentrate, you then need to decide what criteria you are going to use to judge whether their needs were met. For this it would be helpful to read again the section at the end of Chapter 4. As we have discussed before, establishing the criteria for this type of exercise is a difficult task. Some of the obvious possibilities in this case include: economic progress; administrative efficiency; a more humane system; a strong and efficient army.

The third question is another example of the type which looks very complicated, but which can quite easily be broken down into manageable sections. In this case the easiest avenue of approach is to take the quote and split it into two parts. It is quite reasonable to admit that the Tsar wanted to prevent more radical change. You then need to discuss whether this was his main intention. It could be argued that it was with regard to the serf question, and that it is possible, although much more difficult, to see his other reforms in the same light. What you should not do is to dismiss his reforms as mere 'window dressing'. As a body, they undoubtedly had far reaching effects.

Source-based questions on 'The Reforming Tsar'

1   Local government

Carefully read the extract from Valuev on page 74 and the extract from Wallace on pages 74–5. Answer the following questions:

a)   What reason does Valuev give for not giving the *zemstva* power over 'Imperial taxes'? (2 marks)

b)   Explain 'unitary executive power' (line 2). (1 mark)

c)   What did Wallace find most surprising about the *zemstva*? (2 marks)

d)   What explanation would you offer for Wallace's surprise? (3 marks)

e)   What improvements does Wallace suggest that the *zemstva* brought about? (3 marks)

f)   What drawbacks does the evidence from Wallace have for a study of the effects of the *zemstva* between 1865 and 1881? (4 marks)

2   Legal reform

Read the extract from the Tsar on pages 75–6 and the two extracts from Wallace on pages 76–7. Answer the following questions:

a)   What hopes does the Tsar express for the judicial reform? (2 marks)

b)   Does Wallace's first extract suggest that the reform was successful in making the courts 'just, merciful and impartial'? Explain your answer. (3 marks)

c)   Does Wallace's second extract cast doubt on whether respect for the law was increased by the reform? Does it merely suggest that the courts became 'partial' in another way? If this is so, does this mean the reform necessarily failed in its intention? Explain your answer. (5 marks)

3   Miliutin's diary

Carefully read the extract from Miliutin's diary on pages 79–80. Answer the following questions:

a)   What mood dominates in this passage? (1 mark)

b)   What explanation does Miliutin give for his feelings? (3 marks)

c) What within the passage suggests that Miliutin might be exaggerating? Explain your answer. (4 marks)

d) In what ways does the fact that the Statute on Universal Military Service was published the next year support your answer to question (c)? (2 marks)

CHAPTER 6

Reactions to Reform

1 The Intelligentsia

A major problem with the term 'intelligentsia' is that it simply does not translate in any straightforward way. The intelligentsia were intellectuals. In many ways they were the heirs to the ideals and dreams of the Decembrists. However, they were far from being a homogeneous group. They were the product of the debate between the Westernisers and the Slavophiles (see pages 43–4). Many of them took ideas from both groups. They felt that Russia was dreadfully backward in comparison to the west, and they took much of their inspiration from the west. Yet, despite this, they viewed much of what existed in the west as morally reprehensible. They felt that western society corrupted relations between people by emphasising the materialistic aspects of life, thus degrading the quality of life by introducing artificial and legalistic constraints.

The nature of the intellectuals was crucial to their development. Berlin argues that the one thing which characterised the intelligentsia above all else was their search for absolutes. They were almost fanatical in their quest for 'truth' as they defined it. They tended to take ideas and carry them to what often appears to the present-day observer to be a ludicrous extreme. To stop short of what was believed to be the logical conclusion was seen as a sign of moral cowardice. They saw this type of compromise as a characteristic of western civilisation to be condemned. Such extremism was reinforced by the almost incestuous nature of their groups.

The philosophical circles of the 1850s and 60s involved hundreds rather than thousands. Even the 'Populism' of the 1870s embodied thousands rather than tens of thousands. How then could the intelligentsia be important? They tended to set the intellectual tone, which, if not adopted by large numbers of people, was often taken to reflect those who wanted to change institutions. It must be remembered just how small the literate, interested body of Russians was at this time. The total circulation of all the major periodicals was a mere 12,000. The vast majority of Russians were still illiterate and therefore did not even have access to philosophical debate. The intelligentsia thus had an influence out of all proportion to their numbers. Their small size was reflected in the size of the revolutionary groups which developed from them in the 70s. Lack of numbers made them all the more desperate when they faced disillusionment at their failure to politicise the 'masses' and as they came under increasing threat from the authorities. This desperation made them all the more dangerous.

* Perhaps the most famous of the intelligentsia at the beginning of

the 1860s were Bakunin, Chernyshevsky and Herzen. Bakunin was almost an anarchist. He began with a crushing attack on the tyranny of dogma over the individual, and ended with a demand that his own dogma of the superiority of the simple peasant be rigidly adhered to. Herzen was in exile in London, but continued to edit an influential periodical, *The Bell*. He was intent on modernising Russia. For the most part this also meant he was intent on overthrowing the existing political and social system. Yet on occasion he seemed actively to support the Tsar. Like Bakunin he believed in the superiority of the peasant. At first he congratulated 'the Tsar-Liberator' on emancipation. 'Alexander II has done much, very much; his name already stands higher than any of his predecessors.' Within months however, he was bitterly criticising the same Tsar:

1 Oh, if only my words could reach you, tiller and sufferer of
  Russian soil . . . You still believe in the Tsar and the Bishops . . .
  Don't! The Tsar is on the side of the landowners. They are his
  kind of people . . . Through his phoney emancipation the
5 Emperor has shown himself in his true light to the people . . .
  [and then ordered] shootings and floggings.

Where Bakunin advocated anarchy, Herzen advocated a type of socialism based on the *mir*. Through this means he hoped to avoid the excesses, as he saw them, of capitalism in the west.

Chernyshevsky was perhaps even more influential. He was a student of revolution who placed his faith in the *narod* (the people). He contributed to *The Contemporary*, the most popular journal amongst the radical intelligentsia. His views are perhaps best summed up in the following passage:

1 Democracy, by its very nature is antithetical to bureaucracy. It
  requires that every citizen be independent when it comes to his
  personal affairs, and every village and town, every district free to
  manage its own affairs. Democracy requires that the administra-
5 tor be fully accountable to the inhabitants of the constituency
  with which he is concerned . . . Democracy means self-
  government and implies a federal system.

The key element here is individual freedom. He sought a voluntary association of self-governing units, right down to the village. Chernyshevsky lived inside Russia and was arrested in 1862. Whilst in gaol he wrote *What is to be Done?*, which embodied his ideas for a socialist state. It enjoyed considerable popularity, especially with the young. The long-term significance of this work can be seen from the fact that Lenin took the title for one of his own major works.

Finally, it is important to realise that the rejection of what actually existed in the west by the radical intelligentsia was shared by their more conservative counterparts. The following passages are from Aksakov, a prominent Slavophile, and from Herzen. They both show, from very different standpoints, a similar love of Russia and things Russian, but demonstrate a distinct antipathy towards what they saw in the west. Addressing the French nation Herzen stated:

> 1 Russia will never be protestant [moderate and materialistic]. She will never be mediocre [prosaic and middle class]. Russia will never make a revolution just to get rid of the Tsar and replace him by tsar-representatives, tsar judges, tsar policemen.

Aksakov similarly castigated the west:

> 1 Look at the West! Its nations having abandoned the path of religious and spiritual development have fallen prey to the impulse of selfish political vanity . . . They have created republics, have tinkered with all sorts of constitutions and have become
> 5 spiritually impoverished.

It did not bode well for Russia's future development that representatives, on both the left and the right of the spectrum of informed thought, could dismiss so thoroughly what had taken place in the west. The spirit of compromise did not exist. This was of particular importance because the intelligentsia did not have a practical outlet for their aspirations. There was no national assembly or forum in which they could express their ideas. They had nowhere to go. They were held at a distance from the Tsar and the government of their country. They became frustrated and increasingly disenchanted with their position. Some practical outlet for their energies might well have blunted the theoretical edge of the majority of their members. As it was, such an outlet could not or would not be provided. What then was the fate of the intelligentsia?

2   From Intelligentsia to Peaceful Revolutionaries

In May 1862 a number of pamphlets were issued including the very radical *Young Russia*, which called for wholesale changes in the nature and makeup of the state. In June a series of fires in St Petersburg culminated in a major outbreak which destroyed over 2000 shops. It was never proved that the fires were started deliberately, but it was strongly rumoured that either the Poles or the radicals or both were responsible. Whatever the truth of the matter, the fires seriously worried both the authorities and the Tsar.

The publication of leading radical journals was temporarily suspended. A special commission was set up to investigate the supposedly revolutionary organisations. It was expected that they would uncover a secret and pernicious organisation. Their most serious finding was that the Sunday-school movement was apparently a danger to the state. The Sunday schools were duly closed. But the Polish revolt in 1863 led to a growth in nationalist feeling and a decline in radicalism. Herzen, who took a stand on the side of the Poles, lost much of his support and readership of *The Bell* fell sharply.

Though the radicals may have been in decline, demands for constitutional change did not end. The *zemstvo*, set up in 1864, began to channel calls for reform. In 1865 the St Petersburg *zemstva* called for the establishment of a central *zemstva* office. When this met with little response they repeated their request more forcibly the next year. The Tsar felt unable to comply with the request, as he explained:

1 And now I suppose that you consider that I refuse to give up any of my powers from motives of petty ambition. I give you my imperial word that, this very minute, at this very table, I would sign any constitution you like, if I felt that this would be for the
5 good of Russia. But I know that, were I to do so today, tomorrow Russia would fall to pieces.

From his other correspondence there is every reason to believe that Alexander was sincere in his belief. Given the great changes that had already been introduced and the attempt which was to be made on his life in 1866, his feeling was perhaps understandable, though not necessarily accurate. He acted according to his best judgement and dissolved the St Petersburg assembly. The most prominent figures were exiled. This did apparently quieten down demands for constitutional change from the *zemstva*. Yet it also missed an opportunity to bring into the decision-making process many who would probably have strongly supported the Tsar. As it was they were left on the outside of events with an increasing sense of frustration. This led to many seeking an outlet for their frustration in the radical groups.

The impact of one assassination attempt must have been considerable. But the very next year, in 1867, another attempt was made on Alexander's life. This time it took place in Paris and was carried out by a Pole. Not surprisingly, Alexander felt in need of more security. This gave those who felt that a firmer policy was required their chance. Shuvalov, the new head of the Third Section became increasingly important to the Tsar and persuaded him to appoint several new ministers. The Tsar began to retreat from public life, encouraged by his growing liaison with Catherine Dolgoruky (see page 98) which increasingly alienated him from many of his circle. It also gave Shuvalov more power. This reactionary force, coupled, as some saw it, with the lack of any major new reforms, led to a gradual growth in revolutionary activity. As yet, however, it was still largely peaceful in form.

In 1869 Herzen sent out an impassioned plea for activists to go out to the people. In 1871 Sergei Nechaev, who had been in Switzerland with Bakunin, returned to St Petersburg. He was dedicated to active revolt, but a scheme to tie other colleagues more closely to him – by persuading them to murder one of their number as a supposed spy – backfired and he was imprisoned. Between 1869 and 1872 a more successful group of young revolutionaries known as the 'Chaikovsky Circle' became established in St Petersburg. This group was dedicated to putting forward propaganda. Its members did not believe that the peasants were yet ready for an uprising. They founded a secret press and began to distribute pamphlets and banned books, pressing forward with the 'to the people' approach called for by Herzen. They were the forerunners of the *Narodnik* (Populist) movement.

'To all great conquerors' – painting by Vereschagin 1871. (Vereschagin and other painters took their work 'to the people' through public exhibitions of paintings.)

The *Narodnik* movement was quite spectacular, both as a movement and in terms of its failure to achieve its aims. The summer of 1874 saw several thousand students and sympathisers descend on the countryside in the first really major 'movement to the people'. They met with very little success. For the most part the peasants simply could not understand what these strangers from the towns – dressed largely as peasants, which they obviously were not – wanted. When they did understand, they were more likely to denounce them to the authorities than to be converted. Some 800 were arrested, and eventually two groups of 193 and 50 were held for trial.

Undeterred by this setback, the *Narodnik* movement tried again in 1876. This time, however, they dressed as officials or teachers to try and gain the respect and attention of the peasants. But they met with the same result. They then retired to the cities to reconsider their strategy. In 1877 they formed a new organisation – 'Land and Liberty'.

3   The Growth of the Revolutionaries: Vera Zasulich and Catherine Dolgoruky

So far the revolutionaries had enjoyed remarkably little success. One is even tempted to suggest that, had it not been for the actions of others, they might have faded into obscurity at this point. There is certainly no reason to suppose that they were about to make significant gains in terms of support. Yet this is what they did. The initial reasons for these gains lie not in the activities of the revolutionaries, but in the activities of the government. Firstly, the government decided to prosecute those held in prison from 1874.

This proved to be a disaster. It gave the revolutionaries exactly what they wanted – nation-wide publicity. Two famous trials took place. They were actually called the trial of 'the 50' and the trial of 'the 193'. The second trial lasted from October 1877 to January 1878. The defendants took the opportunity of making long, impassioned and well reported speeches bitterly criticising the government and the regime. The idealism and integrity of the defendants made a great impression on both the public and the jury. Of the 193 standing trial, 153 were acquitted. Even those who were convicted were given relatively light sentences. It was a grave shock to the Tsar and the government. Worse was to come however.

* The sentences were announced on 24 January. The next day Vera Zasulich fired a revolver at General Trepov, the Governor of St Petersburg. Trepov had given orders that an imprisoned student be flogged for refusing to salute. Zasulich took matters into her own hands and shot and seriously wounded the General. She was duly brought to trial. Zasulich was the daughter of an army officer. She was a member of 'Land and Liberty' but was actually not in favour of unrestricted violence. She argued that she had acted out of a deep and just sense of moral outrage. Again she made a great impression on both jury and public alike. In April she was acquitted, against all the evidence.

It was not just the fact that she was acquitted that came as a shock, but the manner of her acquittal. When the verdict was announced, there was tumultuous applause from the spectators, who represented a good cross section of St Petersburg society. Moreover the large crowds waiting outside prevented her from being rearrested. She was able to slip away to exile in Switzerland. These two cases made the government look both incompetent and, perhaps worse, impotent. It is difficult to overstate the importance of these trials, although those *émigrés* who claimed that without the Zasulich case there would have been no revolution came close to doing so. The outcome of the trial had a major impact both on public opinion and on the actions and attitude of the government.

   * The government immediately announced that all cases of 'resistance to the authorities, rebellion, assassination or attempts on the lives of officials' would henceforth be dealt with by special courts. Never again would they risk the open courts. However, the damage had already been done. The revolutionaries were not slow to take advantage of the change in the public mood. In the summer, political prisoners in St Petersburg went on hunger strike. Some of them died. In 'reprisal' for their deaths, General Mezentsev, the head of the Third Section in the city, was killed in broad daylight in the middle of St Petersburg. 'Land and Liberty' issued a pamphlet entitled *A Death for a Death*. What was worse was that Kravchinski, the assassin, made good his escape with little apparent problem. Once again the authorities looked and indeed were powerless. Other violent acts followed, including the assassination of Prince Kropotkin, and for the most part the perpetrators escaped.

   It was perhaps this fact which worried the government and the Tsar most of all. These revolutionaries would not have escaped so consistently if any significant proportion of the population had been firmly behind the government. However, if not actually behind the revolutionaries, the mass of the people were either apathetic or sympathetic to them. Even some *zemstva* were involved in secret negotiations with 'Land and Liberty' to try to bring pressure to bear to achieve constitutional reform. The Tsar's position was not helped by what was seen as a dismal diplomatic defeat at the Congress of Berlin (see page 125). The public had expected a glorious triumph; they received an ignominious reverse.

   * In many ways the year 1878 was a watershed. The changes in attitudes and expectations which took place between 1876 and 1879 can clearly be detected in the following extracts from Miliutin's diary:

1 *April 15, 1876* . . . The sovereign often displays a fine trait of character: he magnanimously makes concessions, sacrificing his own pride, when he recognises that this is necessary for the welfare of the state. There is a great deal of gentleness and
5 flexibility in his character and behaviour . . .
   April 26, 1877 . . . Moscow greeted the sovereign, as was to be

expected, with indescribable enthusiasm. Despite the drizzling rain, every street right up to the Kremlin Palace was jammed with masses of people ... the entire square resounded with loud
10 shouts of unfeigned enthusiasm.

July 22, 1878 ... Public opinion in Russia is in an extremely hostile frame of mind toward the government, particularly in Moscow. The Treaty of Berlin arouses almost general displeasure ... They expected something colossal and when the hopes of the
15 idealists were not realised, when the practical reality appeared, everyone raised a cry against our diplomacy and against the whole government ... It is a pity that our not very numerous men of public affairs rarely possess political tact; by getting carried away in their enthusiasm they almost always injure the cause they
20 serve.

April 20, 1879 ... It must be acknowledged that our entire government structure demands basic reform from top to bottom. The structure of rural self-government, of the *zemstva*, of local administration in *uezdy* and *guberniias*, as well as of institutions on
25 the central and national level – all of them have outlived their time; they should all take on new forms in accordance with the spirit of the great reforms carried out in the sixties. Such a task is beyond the powers of our present statesmen ... The higher echelons of government are intimidated by the impudent displays
30 of socialist propaganda ... and think only of protective police measures ... The disease appears and the government imposes a quarantine, without undertaking anything aimed at healing the disease itself ... I am convinced that the present men [in government] are powerless, not only to solve the imminent
35 problem, but even to understand it.

It would be difficult to find a clearer insight into the changing atmosphere within Russia at this time. Miliutin, as Minister of War, was at the centre of affairs during this period. At times one can almost feel the despair and frustration of the author. These feelings were to a large degree shared by the Tsar. When told that someone had strongly criticised him he is reported to have replied:

1 Strange, I don't remember ever having done him a favour; why then should he hate me? Yes, that is what I have learned from bitter experience; all I have to do to make an enemy is to do them a service.

Whilst this may be apocryphal one can understand the sentiments expressed.

  * Alexander was increasingly isolated from official society and even from his son. His liaison with Catherine Dolgoruky was by now public

knowledge. From the beginning of their relationship in 1866, it had caused him severe problems. He was old enough to be her father and had known her since she was ten. Critics saw the relationship as indecent and unbecoming. The fact that he stayed faithful to her, had several children by her, and indeed doted on the oldest boy, George, only made matters worse. She and her children were now moved into the Winter Palace to make it easier to protect his life. It was common knowledge that he intended to marry her as soon as the ailing Empress died. The sympathies of society lay firmly with the Empress. Catherine, however, was soon to play a vital part in the final act of the Tsar's reign. She was of liberal persuasion and possessed an acute political mind. She became the Tsar's closest adviser in the last three years of his life.

4   The Final Act

In April 1879, without the consent of 'Land and Liberty', another unsuccessful attempt was made on the Tsar's life. This attempt prompted the break-up of the organisation. It split into two factions: 'The Black Partition Group' and 'The People's Will' (*Narodnya Volya*). The former favoured peaceful methods and partition of the black soil provinces amongst the peasants. The latter group favoured terrorist methods.

Narodnya Volya was led by an able and intelligent organiser named Mikhailov. He managed to plant a spy in the Third Section. This enabled him almost completely to outmanoeuvre the nation's security police. He even discovered and 'removed' a spy through which the police had infiltrated his organisation. In September 1879 *Narodnya Volya* formally condemned the Tsar to death and set about implementing its sentence. It was known that the Tsar was to return from the Crimea by train in December. Elaborate plans were made. Three separate bombs were to be exploded. The Tsar missed the first by taking an alternative route. The second failed to explode. The third exploded but under the wrong train. The Tsar escaped injury, but, more significantly, the terrorists escaped capture. Three days later *Narodnya Volya* published a public appeal stating that they would spare the Tsar's life if he would agree to call a Constituent Assembly. The offer was pointedly and predictably ignored. However, the Third Section still had little idea who were the leading figures in *Narodnya Volya*.

Mikhailov did not give up. He had managed to infiltrate the Winter Palace itself with a carpenter. Despite the fact that the German government specifically warned that another attempt was imminent and even pointed to infiltration of the Palace, the security police could find nothing. In mid-February 1880, an explosion rocked the Palace. It took place below the dining-room. Yet again the Tsar escaped injury, though some 40 Finnish soldiers died. There was virtually no public reaction.

Such attempts had become commonplace. The German ambassador noted that 'One is tempted to regard as moribund a social body which fails to react to such a shock'.

* However, the Tsar did react, as did those close to him. Catherine encouraged him to try to win back the hearts of the people. Both Valuev and Constantine made proposals for constitutional bodies. These were fiercely opposed by the Tsarevich (Alexander's eldest son) and were not taken up. However, even the Tsarevich realised that something must be done. He proposed that a Supreme Commission be set up to deal with the problems faced by the government. The compromise was agreed. The Tsar appointed General Loris, an intelligent and dynamic man, to head the commission. Loris was stern, but of liberal inclination. He would only accept the position on his own terms, which gave him sweeping powers.

Loris immediately replaced a number of ministers bringing in, in particular, Abaza as Minister of Finance. Both Loris and Abaza were known to be in the confidence of Catherine. Loris embarked on a deliberate policy of concessions to 'reasonable' opinion. Political prisoners were released, press restrictions were relaxed, the hated salt tax was removed and the zemstva were allowed to express themselves. The policy began to take effect. However, there was a setback to this progress in mid-summer. The Empress died in June. After 40 days (the minimum allowed), the Tsar insisted on marrying Catherine Dolgoruky against all advice. Understandably this was seen by many as indecent haste, but the affair was soon forgotten by the majority, if not by the Tsarevich, who felt that his mother's memory had been insulted.

* As the year drew to a close, Loris appeared to be succeeding on all counts. A member of *Narodnya Volya* had finally been captured and tricked into revealing many secrets. Numerous arrests followed and the terrorist organisation was reduced to a very few, increasingly desperate, men and women. Plans were laid for a final attempt on the Tsar's life. Then on Friday, 11 March 1881, Zheliabov, the remaining leader of the terrorists, was captured. He refused to answer questions but boasted that his arrest would not prevent the assassination of the Tsar.

Both Loris and Catherine knew that the situation was becoming increasingly dangerous. The terrorists were almost certain to make one last attempt before they were all rounded up. For the past month Catherine had persuaded the Tsar not to attend the Sunday parade. On Saturday, 12 March, Loris visited the Tsar to outline his proposals for constitutional change. These involved the setting up of two special commissions, made up of interested parties including elected representatives, to prepare new legislation covering economic and administrative reform. He also implored the Tsar not to go to the Sunday parade the following day.

The next day the Tsar again saw Loris and signed the proposals. Having done so he went to the parade. He felt he had been failing in his duty to his people by not attending. After the parade he visited Catherine and told her that he had sanctioned Loris's proposals. On the way back to the palace a bomb was thrown at his carriage. He was unhurt but some cossacks in his escort were seriously injured. The Tsar descended from his carriage, presumably to enquire after their plight. He was met by another bomb which virtually removed both his legs. He was taken back to the palace by his brother Michael to die.

It is one of those strange coincidences that on the very day when Alexander finally gave approval to the calling of elected representatives (albeit in a very limited way) to discuss matters of central government – the very thing which had been demanded for so long and which had been resisted for so long – was the day the terrorists finally succeeded in carrying out their sentence of death upon the Tsar.

5   The Significance of Alexander II

The majority of historians would agree that Alexander II's period of rule was of great significance. However, agreement can be reached on little else. Was he the 'Tsar-Liberator'? Was he the unwise ruler who opened the floodgates which led to revolution? Was he the leader who had the chance to implement real and effective reform, but lacked the nerve to do so? Was he robbed of success by his assassin when in sight of his goal? Support can be found for all these views and others besides.

Alexander did implement more far-reaching reform than any of his predecessors, with the possible exception of Peter the Great. He certainly implemented more reform than any of his successors. He abolished serfdom. He established equality before the law, an independent judiciary, trial by jury and he abolished corporal punishment. Both the army and the economy were modernised and revitalised. Bureaucracy and censorship were limited, education and individual freedom were promoted. In short, Russia was transformed from a semi-feudal society into (at the least) a putative modern state. It was an impressive achievement by any standards. In many ways, therefore, he was both a liberator and a constructive reformer.

Did he open the floodgates by forcing too many reforms on a backward nation which could not stand the stresses they entailed? If he did so, it is difficult to envisage how he could have slowed the pace. Emancipation demanded concomitant reform. The existing system was based largely on serfdom, and with that pillar removed other changes had to take place. As it was, for much of his reign the prevailing opinion of the public was that Alexander did not grant enough reform. His father had warned him that emancipation meant revolution. Perhaps he was right. However, it seems unlikely that an ostrich-like approach would have caused the floodwaters to recede. They had surely built up too far to be ignored.

Did Alexander then miss the chance in the early 1860s to grant open

1860

1861   *Young Russia* first published
        Series of fires in St Petersburg

1863   Sunday schools closed

1865

1865   Calls for greater powers for the *zemstra*

1866   Assassination attempt on Alexander II

1867   Second assassination attempt

1869   Herzen calls for a 'movement to the people'

1870

1874   First major *Narodnik* movement

1875

1876   Second major *Narodnik* movement

1877   'Land and Liberty' formed
1877–8   Trial of the '193'
1878   25 Jan – Vera Zasulich fires on General Trepov
1879   Another assassination attempt on Alexander II
1879   'Land and Liberty' splits – *Narodnya Volya* formed

1880

1880   Unsuccessful bombing of the Winter Palace

1881   Alexander II assassinated by *Narodnya Volya*

Summary – Reactions to Reform

democratic government? Should he have instituted greater reform? It does not seem likely that Russia was ready for such a move. Was he robbed of success as he had it in his grasp, by the bomb which killed him? Loris certainly thought that 'one lucky shot' could undo all that he had striven for. This view is perhaps appealing and does contain some truth, but the proposals put forward by Loris, though they would have been a major step forward, may not have been enough to quieten the unrest. It also seems likely that Alexander III would still have clamped down once more on his accession.

Was it then merely that the situation was not susceptible to any form of solution? Was it too late for a peaceful transformation to be achieved? Had Alexander been a more charismatic figure, had he been able to carry the people with him, it is possible that events might have followed a different course. However, he was an autocrat and he did not possess the charisma of some of his predecessors. He was convinced that he had to remain in charge of events if Russia was to avoid revolution. An autocrat's task is a difficult one. The task of a reforming autocrat is the most difficult of all.

Making notes on 'Reactions to Reform'

Your notes on this chapter should concentrate on how and why elements of the intelligentsia became increasingly radical. This involves looking at the changing aims of the various groups. It also involves looking at the context in which these groups operated. Their small size, their own failures and the activities of the government pushed some groups towards assassination as the only logical way forward.

The following headings should help you to organise your notes:

1.   The Intelligentsia
1.1. The nature of the intelligentsia
1.2. Bakunin, Chernyshevsky and Herzen
2.   From Intelligentsia to Peaceful Revolutionaries
3.   The Growth of the Revolutionaries
3.1. The prosecution of the '193'
3.2. Vera Zasulich
3.3. Reactions to the trials
3.4. 1878
3.5. Alexander and Catherine Dolgoruky
4.   The Final Act
4.1. *Narodnya Volya*
4.2. Winning the 'hearts of the people'
4.3. The Tsar's assassination
5.   The Significance of Alexander II

Answering essay questions on 'Reactions to Reform'

This chapter allows you to answer specific questions on the growth of the revolutionary movement, for example:

1. 'Why did Alexander II's reign end in assassination?'
2. Explain the growth of the revolutionary movements during Alexander II's reign?

You can attempt these questions as a largely narrative exercise, showing how the revolutionary movements developed up to 1881. However, this is not the most effective approach. You would be better advised to look at what allowed them to develop and what prompted them to develop in the way they did. This involves looking at inaction by the government, action by the government which actually encouraged the growth of extreme revolutionaries, the limited options open to those who sought change in Russian society (their own weaknesses) and the nature and character of Alexander himself.

This chapter also builds on the previous two. You can therefore use the detail within it for answers to general questions on Alexander II. For example:

3. '"The Tsar Liberator". How valid a description is this of Alexander II?'

For this question you would have to consider the arguments which could support such a description, largely taken from Chapter 4. However, you would also have to point out that this is only part of the story. You would have to assess the restrictive aspects of Alexander's policies as set out in Chapter 5, and the reasons for the growth of the revolutionary movements set out in Chapter 6.

A very slight change in the first title given in this section would also make it a general question on Alexander II. For example:

4. 'Why, despite all his reforms, did Alexander II's reign end in assassination?'

A similar question to this would be:

5. '"Alexander II's reign promised much but delivered little." Discuss this judgement on Alexander II's reign.'

Both these titles require information from all three chapters, but with different emphases. You will have neither the time nor the space to include all the information at your disposal. You therefore need to make an assertion in relation to the title, and back up your assertion with relevant evidence. You might for example argue that:

Alexander II did in fact deliver a great deal of effective reform, but it was not enough to satisfy a small but violent minority of revolutionaries.

or that:

Though Alexander II passed a great deal of reform, he was never prepared to limit his own autocratic powers, which was the final move necessary to make his other reforms effective.

or that:

Alexander II was never prepared to go quite far enough down the road of reform to be an effective reformer.

Drawing on information from all three chapters (4, 5 and 6), try to back up each of these assertions.

Source-based questions on 'Reactions to Reform'

1   Opponents to Alexander II
Carefully read the four extracts from Bakunin, Chernyshevsky, Herzen and Aksakov given on pages 91–2. Answer the following questions:
a)   What do the comments of the four writers have in common with each other? (6 marks)
b)   In what ways do they differ? (6 marks)
c)   Could the Tsar have done anything to satisfy the criticisms put forward by these four commentators? Explain your answer. (8 marks)

2   Miliutin's views
Carefully read the extracts from Miliutin's diary (pages 96–7). Answer the following questions:
a)   What changes in attitude towards the Tsar does Miliutin describe? (3 marks)
b)   Could the Tsar have had any control over these changes in attitude? Explain your answer. (3 marks)
c)   What changes in government structure does Miliutin see as necessary by 1879? How does he justify his views? (6 marks)
d)   What in Miliutin's diary might justify the view that his criticisms of the existing government structure were accurate? (3 marks)

CHAPTER 7

Russian Foreign Policy: From Vienna to the Congress of Berlin

A policy implies a planned series of actions with a purpose. Foreign policy is therefore about a planned series of actions in relation to other countries. To make sense of any foreign policy one must understand the general aims and objectives which that policy seeks to achieve. These aims will always include the protection of the state. Sometimes they will also include a desire to help the governments or people of other countries, but only if this does not harm the interests of the state itself, and usually only if this furthers the aims of the state concerned.

These general aims rarely change. What does change is how the people who make policy decide that they can best achieve such aims. Events inside and outside the country naturally affect these decisions. This chapter is therefore about: what factors affected the formation of Russian foreign policy (internal and external); what Russia's foreign policy sought to achieve; what actions were taken to try and achieve these aims; and what effects these actions actually had in practice. To make sense of these questions it is essential to know exactly where

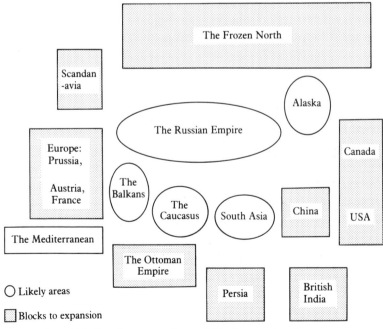

Areas of possible Russian expansion and blocks to expansion

Russia was in relation to other countries and areas of interest (study the map on page 2 and the diagram on page 104 closely, and refer back to them as necessary).

Russia was a European power, but was not *merely* a European power. She also had far wider interests. There is no doubt that the Eastern Question (the future of the Turkish Empire, particularly in the Balkans) was one of the major foreign policy issues for most European powers during this period. Russia was no exception. The fate of Constantinople was particularly important to Russia because she desperately wanted access to the Mediterranean, as her northern ports were closed by ice for part of the year. All three Tsars during this period saw the peace and stability of the rest of Europe as of almost equal importance, though for different reasons. Although Asian interests were less important, they increased in significance as the century progressed, particularly for Alexander II.

Russian foreign policy in this period is naturally often divided in terms of the reigns of the three Tsars. This chapter follows that division both for convenience of study and because there were distinct elements to the foreign policies followed by each of the Tsars. However, there was also a significant degree of continuity between their policies, and this should not be ignored.

1   Alexander I After Napoleon

Alexander wanted a peaceful, stable Europe, just as he wanted peace and stability at home, and he was prepared to compromise in order to achieve this aim. When the Great Powers met at the end of 1814 to determine the shape of post-Napoleonic Europe, they were far from agreed as to what that shape should be. The most difficult problem facing them was Poland. Alexander wanted the complete annexation of the Duchy of Warsaw to Russia, in order to guard his western border. Austria, Britain and France were so opposed to Alexander's demands that they actually signed a secret military convention in January 1815 which was designed to deal with possible Russian aggression should a solution not be found. To the profound embarrassment of the signatories, Napoleon, at the beginning of his famous '100 Days', found a copy of the treaty and sent it to Alexander. It might be reasonable to suppose that sight of this treaty would have had the effect that Napoleon obviously hoped for – a rift between Russia and the other Great Powers. However, for Alexander, there was never any doubt that Napoleon was the greater threat. He made Metternich aware that he was in possession of a copy of the treaty, but stated that he would never mention it again. The revived threat from Napoleon was the spur needed by the powers to solve their differences. The Polish issue was settled with Alexander gaining most (but not all) of his demands.

After Napoleon's final defeat the Great Powers met again, first in

Paris, then in Vienna. Apart from the details of the Second Peace of Paris, these meetings had two major outcomes: the Quadruple Alliance and the Holy Alliance. The former was signed by Britain, Austria, Prussia and Russia. It was the foundation of what became known as the Congress System, according to which the Great Powers would meet periodically to discuss issues of mutual concern. Its basis was that the Great Powers had special rights and responsibilities in the maintenance of international order and stability, and that they therefore also had special rights to intervene in the affairs of other states. The Holy Alliance, on the other hand, was essentially the work of Alexander. It had a very different basis:

1 Their Majesties the Emperor of Austria, the King of Prussia, and the Emperor of Russia, having, in consequence of the great events which have marked the course of the last three years in Europe, and especially of the blessings which it has pleased Divine
5 Providence to shower down upon those States whose Governments have placed their confidence and their hope on it alone, acquired the intimate conviction of the necessity of founding the conduct to be observed by the Powers in their reciprocal relations upon the sublime truths which the Holy Religion of our Saviour
10 teaches.
　　They solemnly declare that the present act has no other object than to publish, in the face of the whole world, their fixed resolution, both in the administration of their respective states, and in their political relations with every other Government, to
15 take for their sole guide the precepts of that Holy Religion; namely, the precepts of justice, Christian charity and peace, which, far from being applicable only to private concerns, must have an immediate influence on the Councils of Princes, and guide all their steps, as being the only means of consolidating
20 human institutions, and remedying their imperfections. In consequence their Majesties have agreed on the following articles:

1. Conformably to the word of the Holy Scriptures, which command all men to consider each other as brethren, the three contracting Monarchs will remain united by the bonds of a true
25 and indissoluble fraternity, and considering each other as fellow countrymen, they will on all occasions, and in all places, lend each other aid and assistance; and regarding themselves towards their subjects and armies as fathers of families, they will lead them in the same spirit of fraternity with which they are animated
30 to protect religion, peace and justice.

2. In consequence, the sole principle in force, whether between the said Governments or between their subjects, shall be that of doing each other reciprocal service, and of testifying, by unalter-

able good will, the mutual affection with which they ought to be
35 animated, to consider themselves all as members of one and the
same Christian nation, the three Allied Princes looking on
themselves as merely delegated by Providence to govern three
branches of the one family, namely Austria, Prussia and Russia;
thus confessing that the Christian world, of which they and their
40 people form a part, has, in reality, no other Sovereign than Him
to whom alone power really belongs, because in Him alone are
found all the treasures of love, knowledge and infinite wisdom,
that is to say, God, our Divine Saviour, the Word of the Most
High, the Word of Life. Their Majesties consequently recom-
45 mend to their people, with the most tender solicitude, as the sole
means of enjoying that peace which arises from a good conscience, and which alone is durable, to strengthen themselves
every day more and more in the principles and exercise of the
duties which the Divine Saviour has taught to mankind.

50 **3.** All the Powers who shall choose solemnly to avow the sacred
principles which have dictated the present act, and shall acknowledge how important it is for the happiness of nations, too long
agitated, that these truths should henceforth exercise over the
destinies of mankind all the influence which belongs to them, will
be received with equal ardour and affection into this holy alliance.

Alexander was driven by a religious fervour which seems to have
increasingly gripped him after the burning of Moscow by Napoleon in
1812. He believed he was 'the depository of a sacred, holy mission'. He
wished to apply to international relations 'the principles of peace,
concord and love which are the fruit of religion and Christian morality'.
The Holy Alliance was signed by the monarchs of Austria, Prussia and
Russia, and afterwards by all the Christian rulers of Europe with the
exception of Britain, where the Prince Regent gave the excuse of not
being a true monarch. Castlereagh dismissed it as 'a sublime piece of
mysticism and nonsense', Metternich as a 'high sounding nothing', and
from its terms one can see why this view has often been accepted.
However, although the Holy Alliance may often have been derided, it
was important as a symbol. It was a mark of the autocratic paternalism
which was characteristic of the initial signatories in varying degrees.
Over the next ten years the Quadruple Alliance was the focal point of
international diplomacy, but it was the spirit of the Holy Alliance which
came to dominate dealings between the major European powers.
   * The first full congress of the Great Powers was held at Aix-la-
Chapelle in 1818. At Alexander's insistence France was accepted back
into the Great Power 'club' and joined what became known as the
Quintuple Alliance. Alexander actually wanted to create a 'universal
league of sovereigns', but this was rather too much for Metternich and
Castlereagh.

The second congress was called in 1820 at Troppau, to deal with some threatening events. Revolutions had occurred in Spain and Naples, the French King's nephew had been murdered, and there had been an attempt to assassinate the British Cabinet. Alexander was convinced that these events were not mere coincidence. This feeling was reinforced by the news of the Semyonovsky mutiny (see page 22). This threat to order in St Petersburg itself, unexpected as it was, seems to have strengthened the Tsar's resolve to oppose any threat to established order in Europe.

The powers reconvened in Laibach in 1821, with Austria and Russia particularly determined to quell the popular revolts in Europe. It was agreed that Austria should help to suppress the revolt in Naples, but no agreement could be reached in the case of the Spanish revolt. As the powers deliberated, news came of the Greek revolt against Turkey, but it was decided to discuss the issue at a later date. One of Alexander's chief advisers was Capodistrias, a Greek who later became the first elected president of Greece. Many in Russia and Greece expected that Alexander would support the Greek revolt. They were to be disappointed. Even when the Patriarch of the Greek Orthodox Church was murdered by the Turks, he stood firm in his condemnation of the rebels. He was convinced that any successful overthrow of established authority outside Russia might fuel further unrest within the Empire.

When the powers met at Verona in 1822 (with Britain now merely on the periphery of the Congress System), Alexander remained consistent to his professed policies. He offered to supply a Russian army to suppress the Spanish revolt, but was prepared to accept the decision of the other powers, who preferred to see France undertake the task rather than have a Russian army marching across the breadth of Europe. The Congress also condemned the Greek rebels. It would have been difficult for Alexander to support revolt in the case of Greece, and at the same time stand firm against revolt in the rest of Europe. However, it seems likely that he agreed with Metternich, who wrote to him in the following terms concerning the issue:

1 A breach opened in the alliance of European monarchs by a war with the Turks, would be a breach through which revolution would enter with rapid strides. The fate of civilization is now in the hands of your Imperial Majesty.

It is easy to dismiss the feelings and attitudes of both Metternich and Alexander as simply reactionary. However, it is important to remember that they had both lived through 20 years of war with revolutionary France, and knew only too well what had happened to many of the French nobility in the first years of the Revolution.

* While Europe remained, as Alexander wished, relatively stable during this period, Russia's eastern frontiers were turbulent. 50,000

troops were employed in controlling the mountain tribesmen of the Caucasus region who were not finally subdued until 1864. Russian troops also advanced beyond the Caucasus as far as Iran. On the unclaimed Pacific border of North America, Russian fur traders had long been established in what was to become California. These traders were coming under increasing pressure from traders from other nations, especially the USA. Alexander was persuaded to issue an imperial decree granting a monopoly to the fur traders and to back up the decree by sending a warship to Fort Ross, some 50 miles north of San Francisco. However, relations between the USA and Russia were good and a compromise was agreed which acknowledged the rights of existing Russian trading posts, but which stated that the land surrounding them was 'unclaimed'. Possible further Russian expansion was pre-empted by the publication of the Monroe Doctrine in 1824, which effectively claimed that the Americas were of no concern to non-Americans. Yet again Alexander was prepared to compromise in order to maintain peace and stability.

2   Nicholas I to 1848

In terms of his foreign policy Nicholas is often described as 'the *gendarme* (policeman) of Europe'. He earned this title. He felt it to be his personal duty to defend Europe against the threat of revolution. He felt that a threat to any legitimate government in Europe was by implication a threat to his own throne. He sought to preserve the Holy Alliance and to maintain Russia's close links with Austria and Prussia. However, Nicholas was not merely another Alexander. To some he appeared rather more brash and direct, to others simply more dynamic. The greater energy that Nicholas displayed in foreign policy can in part be attributed to his early success in this field, and the fact that he came to the throne under the cloud of the Decembrist Revolt (see page 30). Within a short space of time he had achieved what appeared to be two striking foreign policy successes which dispelled much of that cloud.

Against Metternich's wishes, Nicholas concluded an agreement with Britain in 1826 which aimed to put pressure on Turkey to grant Greece autonomy. France joined this agreement in 1827. The Turkish Sultan had employed the help of Mehemet Ali, the Pasha of Egypt, against the Greeks. This had swayed the balance in favour of the Turkish forces, and the Sultan was not inclined to give up what appeared to be certain victory. A combined naval squadron containing French, Russian and British ships was sent to Navarino Bay to blockade the Sultan's fleet and to prevent further troops being landed. It seems likely that all that was intended was to increase the pressure on the Sultan. In fact an engagement took place in which the Sultan's Turkish and Egyptian fleets were almost entirely destroyed. This action, the Battle of Navarino, certainly went further than the British had intended. They now withdrew their pressure on the Sultan. However, the damage had been done. The Sultan was incensed. He expelled all Christians from Constantinople and began to prepare for a Holy War against the infidel, represented (as he saw it) by Russia.

In April 1828 Nicholas declared war on Turkey. The French also played a small part and sent troops to Greece. Little progress was made in the fighting which followed. The Russians were unable to take the strong Turkish fortress of Silistria and had to withdraw at the end of the year to the left bank of the Danube. The next year saw a new Russian commander enjoy a series of decisive victories in which Adrianople was taken and Constantinople itself was threatened. The Sultan hurriedly sought peace, which was agreed at the Treaty of Adrianople in September 1829. Understandably Nicholas exacted favourable terms from the Sultan. Russia gained control of the whole Danube delta, established a protectorate over Moldavia and Wallachia and was granted free passage through the Straits. Turkey also agreed to grant Greek independence, which took place the following year.

It might appear that Russia gained a great deal from this treaty. Other powers certainly thought so. However, given the fact that Turkey was virtually defenceless and therefore at his mercy, Nicholas's demands might be seen as relatively moderate. Nicholas did not attempt to take more land from Turkey because land was not his main aim. Above all he sought stability, as his brother had done. He felt that it was necessary to maintain Turkey if a wider European conflict was to be avoided, and judged that greater demands might lead to the complete collapse of Turkey, which might in turn lead to a wider European conflict over who should control the various parts of the former Turkish Empire.

Nicholas wanted time to implement a number of reforms inside Russia. He deliberately used successful foreign initiatives to improve his popularity at home to give him that time, but would not allow these ventures to threaten the general stability of Europe. Russian armies enjoyed an equally successful and less costly campaign in Persia, where Persian Armenia was brought under Russian control in what was in essence an expansionist war.

* 1830 saw a change in the relationships between the European powers. In July there was a revolution in France which brought Louis Philippe to the throne. A revolution in a major power was exactly what Nicholas had sought to prevent, for he feared that any such revolution would spread. In this he was proved correct. In August 1830, the Belgians revolted against the Netherlands and shortly afterwards Nicholas was faced with a rebellion in Poland. The Belgian crisis came close to provoking a European war. Both Prussia and Russia were strongly inclined to support the 'legitimate' rights of the Netherlands. France sought control of Belgium for herself, and Britain sought to defend Belgian independence as preferable to any one major power

controlling the coastline facing her across the Channel. However, none of the powers wanted a return to the destruction which they had endured during the Napoleonic campaigns. Eventually, in November 1831, the five Great Powers agreed to recognise Belgian independence.

These events led Russia, and to a lesser extent Austria and Prussia, to move away from the new regime in France. Nicholas did not view the new regime as legitimate. There was also an increase in tension between Britain and Russia as the gulf between the constitutional and autocratic systems became more clearly defined. Over the next decade this division continued to widen.

In 1833 Metternich engineered the masterly Convention of Munchengrätz between Austria and Russia. The two powers agreed that the Turkish Empire should be maintained if at all possible. The Austrians, at little or no cost to themselves, were given a voice in the future of the Balkans and Turkey. This agreement was followed in 1835 by an agreement between Prussia, Russia and Austria which in effect reaffirmed the determination of the three powers to continue with the Holy Alliance principle of suppressing revolution throughout Europe. Though Munchengrätz was certainly to the advantage of the Austrians, Nicholas also felt it was to Russia's advantage. He wanted stability and order, and, just as he was revising and implementing a clear legal code inside Russia, he wanted to establish clear binding agreements to cover likely areas of conflict outside Russia.

The following extract is taken from the 'Separate and Secret Articles' of the Convention of Munchengrätz, 18 September 1833:

1　*Article II:* In signing today's public convention, the two Imperial Courts do not exclude from consideration the possibility that despite their wishes and joint efforts, the present order of things in Turkey may be overthrown; and it is their intention that if this
5　happens it should not alter the principle of unity in Eastern affairs which today's public convention is designed to consecrate. It is understood therefore that, in such an eventuality, the two Imperial Courts will act only in concert and in a perfect spirit of solidarity in all that concerns the establishment of a new order of
10　things, destined to replace that which now exists, and that they will take precautions in common that the change occurring in the internal situation of this Empire should not endanger either the safety of their own States and the rights assured them respectively by treaties, or the maintenance of the European balance.
15　　The present separate and secret articles, having the same force and validity as today's public convention, shall be exchanged at Vienna at the same time as those of the aforementioned convention.

In the period up to 1854, relations between Russia, Austria and

Prussia remained consistently friendly, while relations between Russia, France and Britain varied significantly according to the current perceptions of their ambitions and actions with regard to Turkey. The Eastern Question was, for the most part, the determining factor.

In 1833 Nicholas went to the aid of the Sultan to protect Turkey from the attack of Mehemet Ali. Ali had revolted against the Sultan in 1832 and invaded Syria, and by 1833 was threatening Constantinople. A Russian fleet, with 10,000 troops, was sent to protect Constantinople. This had the desired effect of persuading Ali to settle for his gains in Syria rather than seeking even greater conquests.

Nicholas naturally felt inclined to seek some reward for this action. He sent Count Orlov to Constantinople with full powers to conclude a treaty with the Sultan. This became known as the Treaty of Unkiar-Skelessi. The treaty included little that was actually new in terms of what Turkey would or would not do, but there were widespread fears in both Britain and France that whilst Turkey reaffirmed that she would close the Straits to foreign ships in time of war, there was a secret agreement that Russian ships would still be allowed free passage. In fact this was not the case. The treaty was essentially a mutual defence treaty. Russia would come to Turkey's aid if called upon, and vice versa. As the separate article below shows, Turkey had only to agree to close the Straits in time of war:

 1 In virtue of one of the Clauses of the first Article of the Patent
   Treaty of Defensive Alliance concluded between the Imperial
   Court of Russia and the Sublime Porte [Constantinople], the two
   high contracting parties are bound to afford to each other
 5 mutually substantial aid, and the most efficacious assistance for
   the safety of their respective dominions. Nevertheless, as his
   Majesty the Emperor of all the Russias, wishing to spare the
   Sublime Ottoman Porte the expense and inconvenience which
   might be occasioned to it, by affording substantial aid, will not
10 ask for that aid if circumstances should place the Sublime Porte
   under the obligation of furnishing it, the Sublime Ottoman Porte,
   in the place of the aid which it is bound to furnish in case of need,
   according to the principle of reciprocity of the Patent Treaty,
   shall confine its action in favour of the Imperial Court of Russia to
15 closing the strait of the Dardanelles, that is to say, to not allowing
   any foreign vessels of war to enter therein under any pretext
   whatsoever.
      The present Separate and Secret Article shall have the force
   and value as if it was inserted word for word in the Treaty of
20 Alliance of this day.

This was all that Nicholas really wanted – to close the possible avenue of attack from the south. He had no desire to rely on the Sultan's decidedly ineffective troops. Nonetheless, both Britain and France believed that there was more to the treaty than this. In one sense they were obviously correct, as Turkey was now more dependent on Russia for her continued existence. They understandably felt that, to safeguard their own interests, they should do all in their power to limit Russian influence with the Sultan. Their ambassadors did all they could to achieve this objective – the British Ambassador was particularly successful – and a very favourable trade treaty was signed between Britain and Turkey in 1838.

Russian influence over Turkey may have been strong, yet it certainly did not amount to control. In 1839 the Sultan decided to subdue his troublesome vassal Mehemet Ali once and for all. But the Sultan's troops were again soundly defeated and Mehemet Ali now had a perfectly legitimate reason for attacking Constantinople. Nicholas declined to come directly to the aid of the Turks, as might have been expected under the terms of the Treaty of Unkiar-Skelessi. Instead he sought a meeting of the Great Powers to decide the issue. He wanted an agreed international solution to the problem and above all he did not wish to become involved in a conflict with any other major European power. The conference was a particularly astute move. Nicholas had always feared the close alliance of France and Britain. In this conflict France sided with Mehemet Ali while Britain sided with the Sultan. Nicholas, and his chief adviser Nesselrode, saw a way of improving relations with Britain, and at the same time driving a wedge between Britain and France. Nicholas's main aims were to maintain peace and stability in Europe, to prevent the development of a threat to Russia, and thus to allow for uninterrupted progress inside Russia, particularly in the economic sphere.

The following extract is taken from a letter to Count Pozzo di Borgo from Nesselrode in June 1839.

1 The real danger for Europe at large is not in a combat carried on in Syria between the troops of the Sultan and those of the Pasha of Egypt. Neither would there be danger to Europe if the Sultan succeeded in reconquering Syria, as he wishes and hopes to do.
5 The danger would not begin to become serious until, in the event of the fate of arms declaring against the Sultan, the Pasha of Egypt should profit by this advantage to place the safety of Constantinople and the existence of the Ottoman Empire in peril . . .
10 To prevent things reaching such a point, it is of consequence to take measures in time to confine the struggle between the Sultan and Mehemet Ali within certain limits, in order that this struggle may in no case extend itself so as to compromise the safety of the capital of the Ottoman Empire.
15 With this view, it has appeared to us essential to come to an

understanding, frankly, with the Great Powers of Europe who,
equally with us, have at heart to prevent the danger which we
have just pointed out. Among those Powers Great Britain is
incontestably the one that can exercise the greatest influence over
20 the fate of this question, and can co-operate in the most decisive
manner in realising the pacific intentions of our august Master.

The result was the Treaty of London of 1840, by which Austria,
Prussia, Russia and Britain jointly guaranteed the 'integrity and
independence of the Ottoman Empire in the interests of cementing the
peace of Europe'. France was isolated, and realised the dangers of being
so isolated. She therefore joined in signing the Straits Convention, also
concluded in London, in the following year. This convention did not
differ in substance from the treaty of the previous year. Nicholas thus
gave up his position as sole protector of the Turks, but gained a closer
relationship with Britain. He succeeded in weakening the links between
France and Britain which he feared, and gave himself the appearance of
a leader whose primary concern was the peace and stability of Europe.
The appearance was largely justified.

Nicholas visited Britain in 1844 and had detailed talks with the Prime
Minister and the Foreign Secretary. Later in the year he sent Nesselrode to conclude an agreement based on those talks. He was convinced
that eventually the Ottoman Empire would collapse. He felt that it
should be propped up as long as possible, but that detailed arrangements needed to be made with Austria and Britain for when the collapse
came. In what became known as the 'Nesselrode Memorandum'
Nesselrode stated that independent action by the two powers should be
avoided and that joint action was the best hope for maintaining the
peace of Europe. Aberdeen, the British Foreign Secretary, agreed with
the points made and wrote the following to Nesselrode at the beginning
of 1845: 'Your visit to this country gave me the most sincere pleasure'
and 'was attended with no other cause for regret, than that after so long
a separation, I should not have been able to enjoy more of your society.'
This was the high point of Anglo-Russian cooperation. The problem
with Nesselrode's mission was that Nicholas took the agreement to be a
permanent agreement, while the British tended to view it as an
expression of opinion. The Tsar did not take into account the changing
nature and make-up of British cabinets. This misunderstanding was to
contribute to the development of the Crimean War.

3   1848 To the Crimean War

If there was a clear turning point in Nicholas I's reign, it was 1848. Up
to this point he appears to have made real progress inside Russia in
terms of the economy, education, legal reform and serfdom. He had
also helped to maintain order and stability across Europe, and to

maintain close links with the majority of the other Great Powers. In one year much of this was swept away. A severe cholera epidemic and the worst crop failure for 30 years would in any case have caused severe internal problems, but 1848 also saw a surge of revolutionary activity sweep across Europe, in what became known as the 'year of revolutions'.

In France a republic was proclaimed and Louis Napoleon, the nephew of Napoleon Bonaparte, became President. Hungary seceded from Austria and set up a liberal government. Bohemia demanded autonomy, the King of Sardinia was forced to grant a constitution and most of the rest of Italy was in revolt. Representatives of all the German states met at Frankfurt and called for a united Germany. Even in Prussia the King was forced to grant a limited constitution. Inside Russia a supposed conspiracy by 'The Petrashevsky Circle' was exposed by the Third Section.

Nicholas was appalled at these threats to established authority. He resolved to take firm action at home and abroad. At first he intended to send an army to the Rhine to patrol the French border, but his advisers persuaded him against such a move, both on grounds of the cost, and because they felt that it was more likely to lead to war than to prevent it. Nicholas stated openly that if Prussia became a republic, he would send in troops to restore the monarchy. In cooperation with the Turks he put down the nationalist demands of Moldavia and Wallachia. Most importantly, at Austria's request he sent an army into Hungary to put down the revolt there. This allowed Austria to concentrate on containing unrest in Germany and Italy. He also helped to smooth over the disagreements which had developed between Austria and Prussia during the crisis. Nicholas's firm stand was in no small measure responsible for the lack of success enjoyed by the liberal movements in central Europe. At home he instigated a series of repressive measures designed to stamp out any trace of liberal activity.

Within two years both Russia and Europe appeared to be calm once more. However, Nicholas was deeply affected by the events of 1848. It seemed that all he had sought so assiduously to preserve had almost been swept away by what occurred in that year. He became deeply suspicious of any new ideas. In terms of Europe he was particularly suspicious of the new French ruler, Louis Napoleon. Nicholas had viewed Louis Philippe's rise to power in France with deep mistrust, and now to have the nephew of Napoleon as President of a French Republic was almost too much to bear. Louis Napoleon was soon to cause Nicholas problems in a way which he could not have foreseen. In 1852 Louis Napoleon proclaimed himself Emperor of France. Nicholas, already hostile to the new French ruler, refused to acknowledge him as an equal. Louis Napoleon for his part sought to gain prestige at home by success abroad. In a move designed to gain favour with the Catholic establishment in France, he demanded that the Sultan should take the keys to the temple of Bethlehem away from the Orthodox priests and hand them over to Catholic priests. This the Sultan did, although he probably did not understand the possible consequences of such a move.

Nicholas was outraged. It was not merely that the threat came from the upstart Napoleon, but that the threat was to the rights and status of the Orthodox Church. As explained above (pages 9 and 40), the status of the Orthodox Church in Russia was central to the Tsar's position and authority. Orthodoxy was a crucial part of his internal policy. To Nicholas, the handing over of the keys was, in effect, not only a direct insult, but also a threat to the very basis of order and stability in Russia. As the natural protector of the Orthodox Church, Nicholas believed that he had to take firm and effective action. He therefore sent Prince Menshikov to Constantinople to demand that the keys be given back to the Orthodox priests. The Sultan, advised by the western powers (including Britain), refused to do so. Menshikov left Turkey and broke off diplomatic relations with the Sultan.

The following notes were made by Nicholas early in 1853, before Menshikov left for Turkey.

1 *What should be our objective?*
   1. Reparation.
   2. Guarantees for the future. What form can they take?
   3. Conservation of the position as it used to be. Is this probable?

5 *What are the means of attaining our objective?*
   1. Negotiations:
   (a) By letter
   (b) By the sending of an embassy. Advantages and drawbacks.
   2. Intimidation by recall of our mission. Drawbacks.
10 *3.* By force:
   (a) Declaration of war. Drawbacks.
   (b) Surprise by occupation of the principalities. Drawbacks.
   (c) Surprise attack on Constantinople. Advantages, drawbacks; chances of success.

15 *Probable results:*
   1. Turkey will give way.
   2. She will not give way; destruction of Constantinople.
   3. The defeated Turkish army retreats towards Gallipoli or Enos.
   4. Occupation of the Dardanelles.
20 *5.* The French send a fleet and an expeditionary force. Conflicts with them.

Chances of success; possibility of setbacks:
   6. We have the upper hand, Constantinople and the Dardanelles are in our hands, the Turkish army is routed.

25 *7.* Fall of the Ottoman Empire.
  8. Should we re-establish it and on what conditions?
  9. Can we re-establish it with a chance of success?
  10. With what should it be replaced?
  (*a*) Keep all its European territory. Impossible.
30 (*b*) Keep Constantinople and the Dardanelles – disadvantages.
  (*c*) Constantinople alone – an impossibility.
  (*d*) Division into independent provinces.
  (*e*) Re-establishment of the Byzantine Empire.
  (*f*) Reunion with Greece.
35 *Impossibility of both.*
  (*g*) Division between ourselves, Austria, England and France.
  (*h*) What to do with Constantinople?
  11. The least bad of all bad solutions.
  (*a*) The principalities and Bulgaria as far as Kistendji to Russia.
40 (*b*) Serbia and Bulgaria independent.
  (*c*) The coasts of the Archipelago and the Adriatic to Austria.
  (*d*) Egypt to England: perhaps Cyprus and Rhodes.
  (*e*) Crete to France.
  (*f*) The islands of the Archipelago to Greece.
45 (*g*) Constantinople a free city; the Bosphorus Russian garrison;
      the Dardanelles Austrian garrison.
  (*h*) Complete freedom of trade.
  (*i*) The Turkish Empire in Asia Minor.

Nicholas decided to increase pressure on the Sultan by moving Russian armed forces into the Danubian principalities. He specifically stated that he did not seek war. He wanted 'to have in our hands such a guarantee as will insure the re-establishment of our rights in any case'. The threat did not persuade Turkey to give way, mainly because Britain and France supported the Sultan and sent a combined fleet to the Straits in September 1853. The French largely sought prestige, while the British were convinced that Nicholas sought the complete domination or destruction of the Ottoman Empire. In October, Russia declared war on Turkey and the Russian fleet virtually destroyed a Turkish transport fleet at Sinope. Neither France nor Britain felt they could back away from their support for the Sultan. In February 1854 a combined fleet entered the Black Sea, and in March, Britain and France declared war on Russia.

What was to become the Crimean War had begun. Russia was eventually defeated, largely because her armies proved slightly more incompetent than those of the French and British. There was another important reason for Russian defeat, which was even more hurtful to Nicholas. Austria, whom Nicholas justly felt he had 'saved' in 1848–9, adopted a distinctly threatening posture towards Russia. In June 1854 she demanded that Russia withdraw from the Danubian principalities, and went on to station an army of 100,000 men on the Russian border for the purposes of 'observation'. Nicholas was forced to station much-needed troops on the Austrian border to guard against this threat. The Holy Alliance, on which Nicholas had relied so heavily, was conclusively shown to be defunct.

Nicholas died in the middle of the war in February 1855. It was already obvious that the Russian army of almost one million was unable to defeat soundly an invading force of no more than 100,000. Russian weapons and tactics had made little progress since 1815. The supply system was unable even to maintain an adequate provision of ammunition. The new Tsar, Alexander II, was reluctant to admit defeat. In the end it took a virtual ultimatum by the Austrians in December 1855 (which effectively stated that if the Tsar did not negotiate he would also face Austrian troops) to convince him finally that further conflict would be pointless. The powers met in Paris in February 1856, to conclude a peace treaty.

The terms of the Treaty of Paris were not unduly harsh on Russia. The Black Sea was neutralised (no warships of any nation), and the Straits were closed to warships of all nations and opened to commercial shipping, as was the Danube. Russia also had to give up some land to Moldavia. Palmerston, the British Prime Minister, had hoped to deprive Russia of control of Finland, the Caucasus and the Crimea, but the other powers would offer him no support for this policy.

The Crimean War cost nearly half a million casualties. It marked the final demise of the 'Concert of Europe' established in 1815. It also marked the end of the generally accepted view of Russia as the dominant European power. However, its greatest significance was that it made clear to all but the most reactionary Russians, that a radical and thorough overhaul of Russian society was essential. What the war most certainly did not achieve was a lasting solution to the Eastern Question. Even the more optimistic statesmen in Paris in 1856 did not foresee a lasting peace in this area.

4   Alexander II and Europe

The Treaty of Paris (March 1856) brought a final conclusion to the war. The treaty aimed to protect the Turkish Empire against future pressure from Russia. The loss of part of Bessarabia and the continuation of Turkish suzerainty over Moldavia and Wallachia were galling to the Russians, but the neutralisation of the Black Sea was particularly resented because it prevented Russian naval access to the Mediterranean. Of special interest, given the previous efforts of Nicholas I to establish an agreed international system, was the fact that the treaty was incorporated into 'the public law and system of Europe'.

The disastrous defeat in the Crimea convinced Alexander that his chief priorities should be the emancipation of the serfs and a thorough restructuring of the Russian state. He was certain that this was the only way to return Russia to the dominant position she had enjoyed in 1815. His foreign policy was designed at least in part to allow him to do this. Alexander needed success abroad to help deflect internal criticism. He needed to split the alliance between Austria, France and Britain against Russia, to give his reforms time to take effect. He encouraged expansion in Asia which would further economic progress.

* In Europe Alexander sought initially to win over the French and to encourage Franco-Austrian rivalry. This was in part because Russia had felt particularly betrayed by the Austrian threat in 1855, so shortly after Russia had saved Austria in 1848–9. However, there was a more important reason. Stability in Europe was no longer the main aim of Russian foreign policy. It was far more important for Alexander to drive a wedge between his former adversaries. In this he was eminently successful. As he had hoped, war broke out between France and Austria in 1859. However, this break with traditional Russian foreign policy had consequences far greater than Alexander had foreseen, and which he certainly did not hope for. Garibaldi's rising in Italy excited nationalist fervour in Germany, Hungary, Denmark and, worst of all, Poland. There was also a revolution in Greece. Napoleon's support for the Polish cause in 1863 ended the brief period of Franco-Russian cooperation. Both England and Austria likewise supported the Poles, albeit with words rather than deeds. The only ally Alexander could find was Prussia.

Having put down the Polish revolt, Alexander to some extent withdrew from European affairs for the next eight years to concentrate on domestic reform. He allowed the Prussians to redraw the map of Europe and significantly weaken both Austria and France in the process. He followed a conservative policy of avoiding entanglements and he actively encouraged Balkan Christians to submit to Turkish authority. The complete defeat of France in the Franco-Prussian War of 1870–1 led to a Great Power conference in London in 1871. This meeting allowed Alexander to raise the issue of Black Sea neutrality once more. It was agreed that both Turkey and Russia should be allowed to station naval forces on the Black Sea. Thus by maintaining a relatively neutral and conservative stance, Alexander managed to achieve a significant improvement in Russia's position. However, in reality there was a price. Germany was now without doubt the strongest power in Europe. Alexander was understandably determined to maintain close links with Germany. In so doing he set aside his feelings about Austrian betrayal and joined the *Dreikaiserbund* (Three Emperors League) of Germany, Austria and Russia, in 1873. This was little more than a statement of friendly intent, but it can be seen as marking the official return of Russia as an active force in European affairs, dedicated to her traditional role of maintaining the existing order.

5   Alexander II and Asia

Whilst Alexander followed a distinctly cautious policy in Europe, Russia followed a policy of sustained expansion in Asia during this period. The distinction between Alexander and Russia here is deliberate. As one contemporary observer commented:

> 1 A positive fever for further conquest raged among our troops – an ailment to cure which no method of treatment was effective, especially as the correctives applied were frequently interspersed with such stimulants as honours and decorations. Not only the
> 5 Russian generals but even the youngest lieutenants craved after further extension of territory, while those of the officers who were entrusted with any sort of independent command carried into effect their individual schemes. It was, indeed, impossible that such desires should be resisted when by gratifying them it was
> 10 possible for a lieutenant in four years to become a general.

Alexander did not always seem to be fully in favour of the expansionist policy Russia followed in Asia, but it seems likely that this stance was designed to calm the fears of other European powers, rather than springing from any deep-rooted conviction. In any case, expansion was favoured by the military, by two of his closest advisers, Miliutin and Ignatyev, and perhaps most importantly by the demands of the Russian economy which sought new markets and new sources of raw materials. Russian imperialism assumed its modern form in this period, with significant additions throughout Asia. This imperialism was not merely economic in origin. It also reflected the growth of Pan-Slavism inside Russia and the feeling that, as a centre of civilisation, Russia had a duty to bring the benefits of civilisation to all, including the 'barbarian' tribes of Asia.

Seeking some concrete success to offset the humiliation of the Crimea, Alexander certainly did support the final 'pacification' of the Caucasus which had seen continued conflict for the previous half century. The renewed campaign began in 1857 and was finally brought to a successful conclusion in 1864, though only after the majority of the indigenous inhabitants had either been killed or been driven to seek refuge in Turkey. The armies which had pacified the Caucasus were then pointed across the Caspian towards Persia and Afghanistan. Russian territorial control was extended steadily over the next 15 years. In Central Asia the three great Khanates of Khiva, Khokand and Bukhara were incorporated into the Russian state during these years.

In the Far East, Russia negotiated the acquisition of the island of Sakhalin from Japan, with whom she also established trading rights. China was persuaded to cede the territory north of the Amur River as well as the area north of Korea on which the naval base of Vladivostok was founded. Russia gave up only one piece of her territory in the east during this period – Alaska. At the time it seemed of little importance. The fur trade in the area was already declining because the numbers of native otters had been drastically reduced. It was at the extreme edge of the Empire, produced little revenue and appeared to have a low potential for revenue in the days before oil was discovered. It was sold to the USA for $7 million in 1867. The sale was a reflection of the very close relations which existed between Russia and the USA, and of Alexander's desire to maintain those close relations. Though with the benefit of hindsight this sale may be difficult to understand, the fact that Congress almost refused to agree to the sale because they thought that the price was too high, should help to confirm that many contemporaries thought Russia had the best of the bargain.

6   The Balkans and Pan-Slavism

Russia's foreign policy in Europe up to 1870 may be understood largely in terms of conventional diplomacy and interests. However, the problem of the Balkans and the influence of Pan-Slavism did not go away. Pan-Slavism was in part an idealistic movement, but one which had very serious practical implications in that it saw Russia as the natural protector and sponsor of the Slav peoples. It envisaged the development of a federation of the Slavs led by Russia. It was never adopted as an official policy, but it had many powerful supporters in Russia including Ignatyev, the Empress and the heir to the throne. The Pan-Slavs had at least one aim in common with the Orthodox Church: namely the protection of Balkan Christians under Turkish rule.

For the first 20 years of his reign, Alexander managed to control those forces in Russian society which sought direct action in the Balkans. However, 1875 saw the beginning of the first major crisis in the area since his accession. The Slavs in Bosnia and Herzegovina (see map on page 126) rose in revolt against Turkish control. The Turks reacted by implementing a policy of ruthless repression. The Pan-Slav movement inside Russia had not created this situation, but it took full advantage of it by stirring up popular indignation against Turkish methods of repression and by providing financial support to the rebels. Sympathy for the rebels also grew rapidly in Serbia. Russia and the other Great Powers felt they had to intervene before the revolt spread.

In May 1876 the Emperors of Germany, Austria and Russia agreed on a solution, outlined in the Berlin Memorandum, which was very favourable to the rebels. Disraeli felt that the Memorandum went too far, and refused to agree to its proposals, which prevented common action by the Great Powers. The revolt spread to Bulgaria. The Turks reacted with even greater severity. Despite, or perhaps because of, Gladstone's famous speeches about the 'unspeakable Turk', Disraeli continued to refuse to support the break-up of the Turkish Empire in the Balkans. Thus common action by the Great Powers was still prevented. Neither Serbia nor the Pan-Slav movement were influenced by Britain's view of Balkan affairs.

The Pan-Slavs had ensured that the 'Bulgarian Atrocities' aroused widespread public indignation in Russia. They also encouraged the Serbians to believe that they could count on active support from Russia if they went to the aid of their 'Slavic brethren' in the Balkans.

Not all Russians shared this view, as is shown by the extract below from a private letter from Prince Viazemskii, a poet and critic, who had been a friend of Pushkin, and had held several diplomatic posts.

1 Everything that is being done about the Eastern Question is truly a bewildering nightmare. The government is neither seen nor heard . . . All the dams are broken, and the torrent is raging and overflowing on all sides; many are the things it will deluge . . .
5 War at this time may bring us not only harm but ruin. It may drive us into national bankruptcy. Unlike the French, we do not carry billions in our vest pocket . . . Do we really need to sacrifice our bodies, our blood, possibly our future welfare so that the Serbs may prosper? . . . It is better for us to have as a neighbour a
10 feeble Turkey, old and decrepit, than a young, strong, democratic Slavic land that will be wary of us but will never love us. And when have the Slavs been of any use to us? Russia to them is only a milch cow and nothing more. And we let them milk us till we bleed.

However, the Pan-Slavs held sway in Russia, and in June 1876 Serbia and Montenegro, encouraged by promises of support, declared war on Turkey. Thousands of Russian volunteers were allowed to join the Serbian army amidst a wave of popular pro-Slavic sentiment. However, the Russians and Serbians seemed to find it almost impossible to cooperate and the war went badly for the Serbians. With Russian casualties mounting, Alexander was now in a position where he could not abandon the Slavs to the mercy of Turkey even if he had wanted to. In November Alexander made a firm speech which spoke of 'our volunteers, many of whom have paid with their blood for the cause of Slavdom'. He stated clearly that if his 'just demands' for the protection of Balkan Christians were not agreed to by Turkey, and the other Great Powers would not support him, then he was quite prepared to act 'independently'.

   * There followed four months of negotiations between the Great Powers and Turkey which eventually broke down in April 1877. Alexander had wished to avoid war, partly for financial reasons and partly because, since his ill-fated support for Napoleon III, he had sought stability in Europe and generally favoured a cautious and

judicious policy. He now carried out his threat to act 'independently', and declared war on Turkey in April 1877. Even then, it seems he hoped that the Turks might back down, but they did not. Alexander still wished to avoid conflict with any of the major powers and stated clearly that his sole aim was 'the amelioration and security of the status of the oppressed Christian population of Turkey', and that he was sure that he was 'acting in accord with the feelings and interests of Europe'. The war did not go well for Russia, with the Turks providing unexpectedly stiff opposition. Russian forces eventually forced the Turks to sue for peace at the end of January 1878. The Treaty of San Stefano was finally signed in March of that year. This treaty fulfilled the majority of Pan-Slav aims in the area and also significantly improved Russia's position in the Balkans.

Both Britain and Austria felt that Russia had gained too great an advantage from San Stefano and made it clear that they felt it had to be revised. Alexander reluctantly agreed to a meeting of the powers in Berlin. He did so for a number of reasons. First, the war had put great strains on Russia's economy, and, as he had feared, the economy had not been able to bear these strains. It was certainly not capable of sustaining an even larger military effort. Second, despite the success of the war, Turkish resistance had revealed that the Russian army was still far from capable of sustaining a major European conflict. Then, in April 1878, Vera Zasulich was acquitted (see page 95) and it appeared that there was a very real threat of revolt inside Russia. Finally,

Giant Battery before Plevna – the Russian siege only succeeded after six months of fighting and heavy Russian casualties

Alexander did not want, and had never wanted to become embroiled in a major European conflict.

The Congress of Berlin was generally seen as a defeat for Russia, a diplomatic triumph for Britain, and a success for Austria. Russia maintained her gains in Asia, but the Balkan settlement was rearranged in a way which was far more acceptable to Austria and Britain, both of whom had feared undue Russian influence in the region. In particular, Turkish frontiers were redrawn to make them defensible and Bulgaria was significantly reduced in size. Local nationalist feeling was virtually ignored.

In reality the Treaty of Berlin was not a great defeat for Russia. She had recovered control of the mouth of the Danube and had made significant gains in oil rich areas of Asia. The establishment of Bulgaria was still a significant gain and the position of Balkan Christians had been improved. However, inside Russia the Berlin Treaty was seen as a defeat because it was compared to San Stefano rather than the situation in 1876. The Pan-Slavs were outraged and saw the treaty as a betrayal of all they stood for. The Orthodox Church felt it did not go far enough in protecting fellow believers. Russian nationalists saw it as an ignominious diplomatic reverse. The result was to increase the ill-feeling towards Alexander within Russia, which was already running high, and a sustained press campaign against Bismarck and Germany, whom many blamed for the results of the Congress of Berlin. This press campaign itself was partly responsible for the cooling of relations between Russia and Germany, and the fact that Bismarck concluded a separate treaty with Austria in the following year, 1879. The effect of the Treaty of Berlin inside Russia is clearly summarised below in an extract from the diary of Miliutin (The Minister for War):

1 *July 22, 1878* ... Public opinion in Russia is in an extremely hostile frame of mind toward the government, particularly in Moscow. The Treaty of Berlin arouses almost general displeasure. Its cause may be attributed to disappointment. They
5 expected something colossal, and when the hopes of the idealists were not realised, when the practical reality appeared, everyone raised a cry against our diplomacy and against the whole government ... The extravagant speech of Aksakov [a leading Slavophile] before the Slavic Society led first to Aksakov's being
10 ordered to resign the post of chairman of the society, and then to the closing of the society itself. A lamentable fact ... It is a pity that our not very numerous men of public affairs rarely possess political tact; getting carried away in their enthusiasm they almost always injure the cause they serve.

By 1881 Alexander had achieved many of his foreign policy aims. Russia was clearly once more among the Great Powers of Europe, and

After San Stefano

After the Congress of Berlin

was accepted as such, although equally clearly she was no longer the most powerful force in European affairs, that place having been taken by Germany. Russia had made important territorial gains in Asia which had significantly strengthened her economy by giving access to oil and mineral deposits. Alexander had avoided any major European conflict and had strengthened Russia's position in the Balkans. An objective assessment of his achievements might conclude that he had achieved a substantial improvement in Russia's position. However, inside Russia, the majority of his people, whose judgement was of greater importance to the stability of the Empire than that of the rest of Europe, felt that he had failed to achieve the position of eminence and respect in world affairs which was Russia's natural right.

7   Overview

There are a number of different ways of looking at Russian foreign policy during this period. The table below may help to illustrate the changes which took place in her relations with the other Great Powers.

Russia's relations with other Great Powers

★ = Close	+ = Neutral	− = Distant			
Year	*Britain*	*France*	*Austria*	*Prussia*	*Turkey*
1815 (Dec.)	★	★	★	★	★
1820	+	★	★	★	+
1825	−	★	★	★	+
1826	★	★	★	★	−
1827	★	★	★	★	−
1830	+/−	−	★	★	+
1835	−	−	★	★	★
1840	★	+	★	★	★
1845	★	+	★	★	★
1848	+	−	★	+	+
1850	−	−	★	+	+
1854	War	War	−	+	War
1857–60	+	★	−	+	−
1861–70	+	−	+/−	★	+
1871	+	−	★	★	+
1876–77	−	−	★	★	War
1878	−	−	★	★	−

a) Continuity?

There were consistent threads running through Russian foreign policy in this period. The Tsars naturally favoured the maintenance of established governments, especially the other autocracies and monarchies of Europe. They therefore favoured stability in Europe and were generally opposed to change. This was not only because they were autocrats. It was also because their empire was racked by internal problems which meant that any major conflict was likely to fuel internal unrest and place a huge strain on what was a very fragile economy. In Asia, however, the Tsars generally favoured some form of expansion. This was because Asian expansion presented less risks in military terms; offered internal economic advantages via new markets and sources of raw materials; supplied an outlet and training ground for the large standing army; and was viewed in some quarters as a 'civilising mission' thus offering political advantages.

b) The Distinctive Nature of the Tsars' Policies

There were significant variations in policy implementation between the Tsars. After 1815, Alexander I was very much driven by a vision of himself as God's chosen instrument, and, after 1820, by a conviction that all movements for change were a direct threat to the established and proper order, which must therefore be resisted. He sought to establish, largely via the Holy Alliance, an agreed mechanism for dealing with matters of common interest to the crowned heads of Europe.

Nicholas I was more pragmatic, and sought to establish an agreed international code for dealing with such matters, as he did at home with his legal reforms. He also ensured that he was fully involved in all deliberations concerning European affairs, and took a major part in the suppression of the '1848 revolutions' and in limiting their effects.

Alexander II, in order to drive a wedge between Austria and France, abandoned traditional Russian policies and supported French attempts to change the map of Europe between 1857 and 1860. However, French actions resulted in just the type of unrest which his two predecessors had feared, including a revolt in Poland. He then stepped back from European affairs for almost ten years, in the process allowing Germany to redraw the European map. This was not because Russia's interests had changed, or because Alexander had lost interest in Europe, but because he needed time to implement internal reforms and did not feel he could afford to become greatly involved in European affairs. He then attempted to adopt a more traditional policy with regard to Europe. The other significant difference in foreign policy under Alexander II was that Russia adopted a sustained and effective policy of expansion in Asia.

c) Perceptions of Russia

In 1815 Russia was universally seen as the dominant European power.

In 1850 she still appeared to be the paramount force in Europe. Yet by 1856 she was very much at the mercy of the other Great Powers. Then, after a period of relative neutrality in the 1860s, Russia once more firmly established herself as a Great Power by 1878.

However, such brief snapshots only tell part of the story. Appearances here are very significant. How other powers perceived Russian power was crucial in terms of how they reacted to Russia, but these perceptions did not accurately reflect Russia's actual power. In 1815 Russia looked far stronger than she was. Over the next 40 years, although considerable internal progress was made, she suffered a relative decline compared to the other Great Powers. This was clearly exposed by the Crimean War. Significant internal progress was made in the 25 years after 1856, and Russia was accepted back into the Great Power 'club'. However, the weaknesses exposed by the Turkish war in 1877 showed that she was probably incapable of successfully confronting another major European power. This view is strengthened if her internal problems, both economic and political, between 1877 and 1881 are taken into account.

When examining what took place in this period one must remember that there were important differences between Russia's power as perceived by other countries, her power as perceived by her own leaders and her real power. Her internal problems, and her actual ability as judged by her rulers, set limits to what she could and did try to accomplish. The Great Powers' perceptions of Russia at times gave her credit for far greater powers and abilities than she actually possessed. This at times allowed her greater influence than was her due. This difference between perception and reality is crucial when assessing the interaction between states at this time.

Making notes on 'Russian Foreign Policy: From Vienna to the Congress of Berlin'

This chapter describes a number of phases in Russian foreign policy. In each case your notes should concentrate on (i) the context in which given actions took place, both internal and external, (ii) the intention behind the action and (iii) the effects of the action. You should also pay close attention to (iv) the perceptions of those involved and how they affected the course of events. The following headings and sub-headings should help you:

1.   Alexander I After Napoleon
1.1. The peace treaties and the Holy Alliance
1.2. The Congress system
1.3. Russia's wider horizons

Relations with the Great Powers

The Eastern Question

1815 Alexander sets up the Congress System and the Quadruple Alliance. Seeks to annexe Poland to protect Russia's Western Border.

The Greek Revolt

1828 Russia declares war on Turkey

1830 Revolution in France

1831 Belgian Independence

Nicholas fails to persuade other powers to prevent these changes

1833 Treaty of Unkiar-Skelessi

1839 Nicholas decides not to intervene directly against Mehemet Ali

1840   Treaty of London

1848 The Year of Revolutions (Nicholas helps to quell Austrian revolt but has little success elsewhere)

1852   Louis Napoleon becomes Emperor of France

1854–6   The Crimean War

1856   The Treaty of Paris

1857–9 Alexander briefly encourages French destabilisation in Europe

1859–70 Alexander avoids entanglements in Europe and expands in Asia

1870–1   Franco-Prussian War

1875 Revolt in Bosnia-Herzegovina
1877 Russia declares war on Turkey
1878 San Stefano

The Congress of Berlin

(Left margin vertical text:) ALL THREE TSARS DESIRE PEACE — AND STABILITY IN EUROPE

Summary – Russian Foreign Policy: From Vienna to the Congress of Berlin

---

Source-based questions on 'Russian Foreign Policy: From Vienna to the Congress of Berlin'

1   The Holy Alliance
Carefully read the extract from the Holy Alliance (pages 107–8). Answer the following questions:
a)   How far is it accurate to say that Article 1 clearly shows the influence of Alexander I? (4 marks)
b)   Does Article 2 amount to anything more than a statement of religious belief? Explain your answer. (2 marks)
c)   Does Article 3 suggest that the Holy Alliance had a long-term future in Europe? Explain your answer. (4 marks)
d)   How far does a reading of this extract justify Castlereagh's description of it as 'a sublime piece of mysticism and nonsense'? (5 marks)

2   The Convention of Munchengrätz
Carefully read the extract from the Convention of Munchengrätz (page 112). Answer the following questions:
a)   What was the expressed intention of this secret article? (2 marks)
b)   In what ways might such 'secret' agreements be counter-productive? (3 marks)
c)   How far does the fact that this article had to be included in the Munchengrätz Convention at all show that the Holy Alliance was no longer an effective force in European politics? (5 marks)

3   Unkiar-Skelessi and Nesselrode
Carefully read the extracts on pages 113–15. Answer the following questions:
a)   Why was Russia so concerned about who controlled Constantinople and the Dardanelles? (3 marks)
b)   Was Unkiar-Skelessi a defensive treaty from the Russian point of view? If so, why were other powers so concerned about its terms? (3 marks)
c)   In what ways do the two extracts taken together suggest a change in Russia's priorities during this period? (4 marks)

4   Nicholas I's private notes on the Near East – 1853
Carefully read the Tsar's notes on Russia's policy options (pages 117–18). Answer the following questions:
a)   Why might this be considered a particularly reliable piece of evidence about how the Tsar viewed the Eastern Question? (4 marks)
b)   What do these notes suggest about Nicholas's approach to the problem? (5 marks)
c)   Does the whole document suggest that Nicholas wanted to avoid war, but not at any price? Explain your answer using quotations as evidence. (6 marks)

5   Viazemskii and Miliutin
Carefully read the extracts from these two contemporaries on pages 123 and 125. Answer the following questions:
a)   Compare and contrast the views of the two writers on the Slavophile movement. (4 marks)
b)   What was their opinion on the public's view of what was possible? (2 marks)
c)   In what ways do the two extracts help to explain Russia's actions between 1876 and 1879? (4 marks)

6   Between Europe and Asia
Carefully study the Russian map reproduced on page 8. Answer the following questions:
a)   Identify the three groups of horsemen shown as bearing down on Russia from the north-west, the south-west and the south-east. (3 marks)
b)   What evidence does the illustration contain that would allow historians to date it with confidence to a period well before 1815? (3 marks)
c)   What can be deduced about the artist's perception of Russia's international situation? Explain your answer. (4 marks)
d)   Were the attitudes that lay behind the drawing of the map apparent in Russian foreign policy in the period 1814–81? (5 marks)

7   The Portrayal of War

Carefully study the illustrations reproduced on pages 94 and 124.
Answer the following questions:

a)   What message is the artist of 'To all great conquerors' attempting to communicate? (3 marks)

b)   What messages is the artist of 'The Giant Battery before Plevna' attempting to communicate? (3 marks)

c)   Is either painting intrinsically more useful to the historian of the period? Does their value simply depend on the questions to be answered? (4 marks)

Glossary

autocracy   traditional Russian system of government in which all power rested in the hands of the Tsar without any theoretical limits.

Boyar   traditional and hereditary Russian noble – as a class they were effectively superseded by the system of Ranks instituted by Peter the Great in 1722.

Decembrists   a disparate group which planned and led the unsuccessful revolt against Nicholas I in December 1825.

duma   elected town assembly/council set up in 1870 as a counterpart to the *zemstva*.

intelligentsia   blanket term covering a wide ranging group which saw itself as forming an artistic, social and political vanguard in nineteenth century Russia.

mir   village community to which all villagers belonged. It was usually run by a council of elders who decided how land should be distributed and what and when farming activities should take place.

Narodniks   political movement which sought to explain the benefits of a type of socialism to the people, particularly in the countryside.

zemstva   elected councils for local self-government. In 1864 they were set up at the district and provincial level. The nobility dominated these councils, particularly at the provincial level. They were nonetheless generally felt to be a success.

Further Reading

A number of useful and readily available books exist in paperback:

H. Seton-Watson, *The Russian Empire 1801–1917* (Clarendon Press 1988)

This is rather solid, but provides a wealth of detail and analysis.

S. Pushkarev, *The Emergence of Modern Russia 1801–1917* (Pica Press 1985)
J. N. Westwood, *Endurance and Endeavour: Russian History 1812–1986* (OUP 1987)

These are both slightly more accessible surveys of the period.

Richard Pipes, *Russia under the Old Regime* (Penguin 1974)

This provides a stimulating analysis of the development of Russian society.

Maureen Perrie, *Alexander II, Emancipation and Reform in Russia 1855–1881* (Historical Association 1989)

This book provides an admirably brief analysis of the period.

W. E. Mosse, *Alexander II and the Modernization of Russia* (London 1958)
M. McCauley and P. Waldron (eds), *The Emergence of the Modern Russian State, 1855–1881* (London 1988)

Both these books provide a deeper analysis of the period.

M. Falkus, *The Industrialisation of Russia 1700–1914* (London 1972)

This provides a concise, but effective, picture of industrial development.

I. Berlin, *Russian Thinkers* (Pelican 1984)

A book which furnishes the reader with a stimulating analysis of the growth of the intelligentsia and the Populist movement.

Sources on Russia 1815–81

Source collections in translation are rare, but the following are generally available through inter-library loan:

G. Vernadsky (ed.), *A Sourcebook for Russian History from Early Times to 1917*, Vols. 2 and 3 (Yale University Press 1972)

A very comprehensive collection.

D. M. Wallace, *Russia* (London 1912)

Written by *The Times* correspondent in Russia. Later published as *Russia on the Eve of War and Revolution* (New York 1961)

A large number of contemporary novels exist in translation. A possible starting point in this field might usefully be:

M. Sholokhov, *Virgin Soil Upturned* (Pan 1988)
I. S. Turgenev, *Fathers and Sons* (Penguin 1970)

Useful for internation affairs are:

M. S. Anderson (ed.), *The Eastern Question 1771–1923 – Documents* (London 1970)
G. A. Kertesz (ed.), *Documents in The Political History of the European Continent 1815–1939* (Clarendon Press 1968)

Acknowledgements

The publishers would like to thank the following for permission to reproduce the copyright material:

Edward Arnold for the extracts from *The Eastern Question 1774–1923 – Documents* edited by M. S. Anderson; Longman for the extract from *The Making of Russia* by J. Hasler; Penguin for the extract from *Russia under the Old Regime* by Richard Pipes.

The publishers would also like to thank the following for permission to reproduce copyright illustrations:

The Mansell Collection (page 54); The Royal Society of Medicine (cover); The Society for Cultural Relations with the USSR (page 94).

Index